G R Halson, MA

Comprehension, Interpretation and Criticism

In four stages

Introductory book

Second edition

Longman

LONGMAN GROUP LIMITED
Longman House
Burnt Mill, Harlow, Essex

First published 1981
ISBN 0 582 24263 0

*Set in 11/12 pt Baskerville
by Syarikat Seng Teik Sdn. Bhd., Kuala Lumpur, Malaysia*

*Printed in Singapore by
Huntsmen Offset Printing Pte Ltd.*

Contents

Introduction

As the title of this series implies, *Comprehension, Interpretation and Criticism* is not a collection of 'comprehension tests'. Although some of the questions accompanying the passages can be used for written answering, it is hoped that the questions generally will be used more as a basis for class discussion so that pupils and teacher may become involved in a joint exploration of each passage.

In its choice of passages and in its study material the Introductory Book is designed for use with pupils of 11 to 12 years of age, either in middle schools or in secondary schools. It can be used, as books in the first edition of the series have been, with mixed ability groups. The questions have been devised to cover a wide range of ability to respond, in the hope that all members of a group will find the opportunity to contribute to the exploration of the passage. In offering this wide range of questions it is not envisaged that each set of questions will be worked through in its entirety. Even the most carefully formed mixed ability groups within a particular year vary greatly in their group capacity to respond to imaginative literature, and it is suggested that teachers select for discussion those questions which reflect the composition of the group with whom they are working. Generally speaking the Section B questions invite a wide range of imaginative response and some of the questions have been deliberately included to challenge the most sensitive and imaginative (and not necessarily the most able) members of a group. What is important is that the passages and the study material should combine to produce an integrated approach to English studies whereby language studied in the context of its use in literature can be seen to be both a medium for creative expression and a means of precise communication.

The series thus aims to provide a clear link between the

study of language and the study of literature. 'Comprehension' should not be regarded as a language activity to be practised in isolation, and it is to be regretted that, all too often, 'comprehension' passages are regarded as being subservient to the questions which accompany them. Since comprehension in the true sense of the word is the action of taking in or grasping with the mind, questions should be concerned with the *exploration* of meaning and intention. They should perform the function of guiding pupils towards an appreciation of the passage not only at the level of surface understanding of what the passage is about but also at the level of deeper understanding of how meaning is conveyed. One of the advantages of studying passages from literature in this context is that pupils are enabled to focus attention on the importance of language and style in literature more closely than is normally possible when they are reading a complete book. This experience of close-focussing can help pupils towards a greater awareness of qualities not only of language and style but also of character and plot as they extend both their general reading and their literary studies. At the same time it can help them towards a greater awareness of both the imaginative and the precise use of language in their own writing.

The preparation of a new edition of a series provides an opportunity to make needed changes, although the original intentions of the series remain in essence. It remains a strong intention that the passages in each stage of the series should be enjoyable to read and that they should be substantial enough to give each stage the added character of a prose anthology. Closely linked with this intention is the hope that pupils will be encouraged to read the books from which the passages have been taken.

A number of passages have been withdrawn, for various reasons, in the preparation of the new edition of the Introductory Book. Some passages in the first edition are now clearly out of date. Some have, experience has revealed, been too short to engage the interest of pupils fully. Some now appear uncomfortable in their detachment from their parent books. Some, it has been clear, have not suited the reading interests of the age range of pupils for whom the book is designed.

In choosing replacement passages more use has been made of episodes from books written for children by established children's writers – Laura Ingalls Wilder, Mary Elwyn Patchett, Malcolm Saville and Nina Bawden, for instance. Most of the books from which the new passages are taken are regularly available in paperback editions, and details of these editions are given in the section 'Suggestions for reading' following each passage. Such information may be useful to pupils interested in purchasing their own copies at their local or school bookshop.

The supporting material is now divided into four sections, of which Sections A and B are designed to explore meanings and implications in the passage, through discussion.

Section A, 'Comprehension', contains plenty of direct questions which are designed to involve pupils initially in discussion of the *content* of the passage rather than of the language and style. In basic terms these questions are concerned with what happens and why it happens, and with conclusions which can be drawn from direct evidence.

Having looked at the main elements of the content, Section B, 'Interpretation and criticism', seeks to explore the detail of the passage, particularly in connection with language and style. Considerable emphasis is laid on the study of word meanings according to their contexts in the passage. It is vital, both to a pupil's understanding of new words encountered in reading and a pupil's use of new words in his composition, that he should be aware that very often there is no absolute meaning of a word and that a particular context will often determine a particular shade of meaning. The many references to the necessity of using 'a good dictionary' in answering questions are intended to underline the fact that the shade of meaning of a word in its particular context can often not be ascertained from a pocket dictionary. Sometimes it is possible to miss totally an author's purpose in using a specific word unless this is traced through in a dictionary such as the Shorter Oxford, where much can be gained from tracing not only the precise shade of meaning but also the derivation of certain words. This activity clearly requires the help of the teacher. Ideally, one of the most important aspects of Section B is the assessment of the appropriateness of words and phrases in their contextual use and the interpretation of what the writer intends his readers to grasp from his use of specific words and phrases. Such considerations will help to answer the broader questions of how a writer conveys atmosphere or mood, or how he achieves a particular view of a character or a place, or how he conveys sense impressions – of sight, sound, or movement, for example. This section is thus concerned with both the *interpretation* of meaning and the assessment – i.e. *criticism* – of the aptness of language in use or the aptness of a particular style of writing.

For the purpose of this series the word *criticism* is used in the general sense of the assessment of the qualities and character of the writing rather than in its particular sense of the critical science of text study, i.e. literary criticism. For this reason it will be found that the use of the terminology of literary criticism has been deliberately avoided throughout the series, as has the use of open-ended requests to 'comment on the style of the passage'. It is more important at this stage to regard the term 'style' as referring in the most general way to the *manner of writing* and to consider examples of how the style contributes to the clarity and the effectiveness of the content of the passage at *specific* points. Only where it has been considered that pupils can understand the relationship between style and content in a particular passage are questions asked which involve an appraisal of how a writer achieves a particular *total* effect – and there the question is expressed in terms of 'ingredients' rather than 'aspects of style'.

Some questions of the type previously encountered in Section C, 'Comment and discussion', in the first edition, now appear in Section B, where they best belong.

A new Section C, 'Ideas for writing', has been introduced. The concern of so many of these passages with personal experiences would seem to create a suitable imaginative climate for pupils to match these experiences with their own or to seek to establish an imaginative identity with these experiences if there is no real-life equivalent. If the impact of a piece of literature is sufficiently strong, the pupil may welcome an opportunity to create or to recreate for himself through the medium of writing. The section is intended to provide ideas for writing should the inclination to write be present. In such circumstances it will thus provide material for composition, but it is not planned to provide material for composition as a specific *exercise*, and the limitation of ideas to those intended to promote personal or creative writing is thus deliberate.

Section D, 'Suggestions for reading', is a new section, introduced partly to underline the fact that the passages themselves form an anthology intended to give pleasure in reading. It does grave disservice to literature to use it in any comprehension textbook in such a way that the passage merely provides mechanical test material and is then discarded. One hopes that pupils using this book will either want to read more of the books from which the passages are taken or will be interested in sampling other writing by the same author or other writing in a similar genre or on the same subject. In the first edition some references were made to the books from which the passages were taken and to other books by the same author in the 'Notes on authors' at the end of the book. This now seems to be too detached and impersonal, and Section D has been introduced so that specific recommendations can be made in close relationship to each passage. It is not, of course, intended that pupils should feel compelled to follow up the suggestions systematically after studying each passage. Clearly, different types of writing will appeal to different individuals and the suggestions for reading are, in this sense, designed to help pupils to select books which suit their own tastes and interests. Thus, it is envisaged, some pupils may wish to read more of Malcolm Saville's adventure stories after studying the passage 'A shelter from the storm' whilst others may prefer to follow up the real-life adventures in the Laura Ingalls Wilder books. The desirable outcome of Section D is that pupils should feel encouraged to extend their leisure reading into those areas of reputable children's or adult literature which, from their experience of passages in this book, seem to offer interesting prospects. This invites liaison with the school library or local branch library and with the school bookshop or local bookshop.

The 'Notes on authors', which will be found at the end of the book, are now more concerned with details of the writers themselves.

Acknowledgements

We are grateful to the following for permission to reproduce copyright material:

A.B.P. (U.K.) Ltd for an extract from *The Little House in the Big Woods* by Laura Ingalls Wilder published by Methuen Children's Books Ltd; The Bodley Head for an extract from *Magnolia Buildings* by Elizabeth Stucley and an extract from Chapter 1 *Septimus and the Danedyke Mystery* by Stephen Chance; the author's agent for an extract from Chapter 8, *Dolphin Island* by Arthur C. Clarke, published by Victor Gollancz Ltd; Collins/Armada and the author, Malcolm Saville for an extract from *Not Scarlet But Gold* copyright © Malcolm Saville 1962; Constable Publishers Ltd for an extract from *This Time Next Week* by Leslie Thomas; Dobson Books Ltd for an extract from Chapter 2 *A Boy and His Bike* by Richard Potts; Faber and Faber Ltd for an extract from Chapter 2 *Marianne Dreams* by Catherine Storr, reprinted by permission of Faber and Faber Ltd; Victor Gollancz Ltd for an extract from *The Peppermint Pig* by Nina Bawden; Lutterworth Press for an extract from *Ajax the Warrior* by Mary Elwyn Patchett; Oxford University Press for an extract from *The Edge of the Cloud* by K.M. Peyton, 1969, by permission of Oxford University Press; Pan Books Ltd for an extract from *Haunted Houses* by Aidan Chambers; Penguin Books Ltd for an extract from *Jet, A Gift to the Family* by Geoffrey Kilner (Puffin Books, 1979) pp 49-51 Text copyright © Geoffrey Kilner, 1976, reprinted by permission of Penguin Books Ltd; The Reader's Digest Association Ltd for an extract from *Folklore Myths and Legends of Britain* copyright © 1973 The Reader's Digest Association Ltd.

1
A shelter from the storm

Petronella Stirling ('Peter') has been for a morning ride over the wild Shropshire hills on her Welsh pony, Sally. Legend has it that when the rocky summit of the Stiperstones, nicknamed 'The Devil's Chair', is shrouded in mist, then the Devil is sitting up there.

Peter was within a mile of the narrow road which ran under the flank of the mountain when she realised that the uncertain weather was changing for the worse. The Devil's Chair had vanished again in the mists, and the sky to the west was thick and lowering with thundery clouds. Once she reached the road she had only to turn to the left and then, still keeping in the shadow of the mountain, she was only about another mile from Seven Gates[1]. A mutter of thunder in the distance unsettled the pony, who hated it, and Peter had no difficulty in encouraging
10 her to canter. They reached the road before the next crash came and then, as Peter soothed her, the storm broke and the road was white with bouncing hailstones which stung her face and hands and beat about her head until the tears came to her eyes.
   Suddenly she remembered that just off the road near here was a ruined cottage. Jenny had been with her when she had last seen it and had told her that once a witch had lived there, and that it was now so haunted that nobody dared go inside. This remark was typical of Jenny, who had a very vivid
20 imagination and gloated over horrors. Although Peter had never liked the Stiperstones and never would, she had always been rather sorry for witches and, anyway, was sure that her

[1] the farm to which Peter is riding

friend was talking nonsense about this particular place. As her jeans were now wet through and her hair limp and draggled, she felt that she would have faced a coven² of witches if she could only shelter until the storm passed over, and so she urged Sally forward trying, as she did so, to shield her face from the stinging hail.

30   Then the hail turned to rain and, through the grey curtain, Peter saw on her right the shape of the cottage and an outbuilding standing back from the road. There was no gate now, but Peter forced Sally through a gap in the wall and across the wilderness of waist-high weeds which once had been a garden, towards a ruined stable.

Thankfully she slipped from Sally's back and led her into shelter. There was not much roof left, but the far corner under the manger was reasonably dry, and there Peter made a fuss of the pony and quietened her down. Then she realised that there was not enough dry room for both of them in the stable. The

40   rain was still heavy and she could see the water gushing from the broken gutters of the cottage and pouring down its stone walls. There was no glass in the windows and the place looked grim and forbidding. Only at the back had the slates slipped from the rotting rafters so she decided to shelter just inside the front of the cottage.

With a reassuring word to Sally she dashed out of the stable, through the forest of weeds and into the doorway which led straight into a stone-flagged room. Although dry this was a horrid room. Tatters of discoloured paper hung from the

50   walls, the old fireplace was rusty and full of rubbish, while in one corner the ceiling had collapsed leaving a pile of messy· plaster on the floor. In the other corner a door, hanging on one hinge, led into a back room.

Peter sniffed fastidiously and then shrugged out of her heavy knapsack. Her mack was rolled on top but she had not had time to put it on and was in a sorry mess. She took off her leather jacket and shook it, and then looked ruefully at her soaked jeans. They were very uncomfortable, but she had just decided that they might as well dry on her when she heard,

60   above the roar of the rain, the crunch of a step behind her. For a moment, remembering Jenny's fears and certainty that this

---

² gathering

place was haunted, she stood stock still, staring at the rain slanting down outside the window. She stifled a scream which rose in her throat and then, with a hand to her mouth, she found the courage to turn round.

MALCOLM SAVILLE
Not Scarlet but Gold

A Comprehension

1 What advance warning did Peter have of the approaching storm before it broke?
2 For what reasons did Peter decide to seek shelter in the ruined cottage?
3 Why was she not bothered about Jenny's story of the cottage's being haunted?
4 What were Sally's reactions to the storm?
5 How could one tell, approaching the cottage, that it was no longer lived in?
6 What evidence is there in the passage of Peter's concern for Sally both before and after they reached the cottage?
7 What shelter did Peter find for Sally and for herself at the deserted cottage?
8 What evidence is there in the passage that the cottage is probably too decayed to be made liveable in again?
9 For what reasons, do you think, did Peter's thoughts quickly turn to Jenny's story about the cottage, when she heard 'the crunch of a step behind her' (line 60)?
10 What impressions of Peter as a person do you gain from reading this passage?

B Interpretation and criticism

11 (a) What is the difference between a 'canter' (line 10) and a 'trot'?
   (b) Why did Peter encourage Sally to canter at this point?
12 How might Jenny look and speak when she 'gloated over horrors' (line 20)?
13 What would hair look like when it is described as 'draggled' (line 24)?

3

14 What exactly *is* 'the grey curtain' referred to on line 29?

15 Why does the writer describe the water as '*gushing* from the broken gutters' (line 40) rather than as 'flowing'?

16 What does the word 'tatters' (line 49) suggest about the state and the appearance of the wallpaper?

17 (*a*) What made Peter sniff 'fastidiously' (line 54)?
    (*b*) What sorts of habits and behaviour would you associate with someone who is a 'fastidious' person?

18 What kinds of movement would be involved when Peter '*shrugged out* of her heavy knapsack' (line 54)?

19 (*a*) What special qualities do the words 'roar' and 'crunch' (line 60) each possess?
    (*b*) Why, in this case, would the step of the approaching person 'crunch', do you think?

20 (*a*) What does the word 'slanting' (line 63) tell you about the way the rain was falling?
    (*b*) Can you explain why the rain would be 'slanting', bearing in mind how stormy it was outside?

21 (*a*) What *typical* ingredients of the thrilling adventure story can be found in this passage?
    (*b*) How does the writer make full use of these ingredients to lead up to an exciting climax?

C *Ideas for writing*

22 The surroundings and the insides of some buildings, particularly ruined or deserted buildings, can often create a rather frightening atmosphere. Think carefully about such buildings in your home area. Which do you find somewhat scarey to visit, and why? Discuss these in class, and then write a story about one of them and about your adventures there, imaginary or – maybe – real!

23 The passage you have just been reading leaves off at a most exciting moment. Why not continue the story yourself? Carry on writing from where this extract ends. Who is entering the cottage? What happens next? How does Peter get home safely – if she does?

D *Suggestions for reading*

This passage comes from Malcolm Saville's adventure novel

Not Scarlet but Gold – the words of the title being the clue to the treasure which is at the heart of the adventure. The book is one of a number of exciting books by Malcolm Saville which feature the Lone Pine Club, a secret society of teenagers formed at a lonely house called Witchend in the Shropshire hills. An interesting aspect of these Lone Pine stories is that they are set in *real* countryside – an area of wild moorland and rocky hilltops which always plays a dramatic part in the stories and which you can perhaps visit for yourself after reading the books.

The 'Lone Pine' adventures, published first in hardback by George Newnes Ltd, have been published in paperback by Armada Books. They include *Mystery at Witchend, Saucers Over the Moor, The Secret of the Gorge, Mystery Mine*, and *The Man with Three Fingers*.

A very unusual adventure story, also set in real countryside around Alderley Edge in Cheshire, is *The Weirdstone of Brisingamen* by Alan Garner, published as an Armada Lion paperback.

2
On the edge of
the Great Barrier Reef

At last they reached the edge of the reef and stood looking down into the gently heaving sea. The tide was still going out, and water was pouring off the exposed coral down hundreds of little valleys it had carved in the living rock. There were large, deep pools here, open to the sea, and in them swam fish much bigger than any Johnny had seen before.

'Come along,' said Mick, adjusting his face mask. With scarcely a ripple, he slipped into the nearest pool, not even looking back to see if Johnny was following him.

10   Johnny hesitated for a moment, decided that he did not want to appear a coward, and lowered himself gingerly over the brittle coral. As soon as the water rose above his face mask, he forgot all his fears. The submarine world into which he had looked from above was even more beautiful, now that he was actually floating face down on the surface. He seemed like a fish himself, swimming in a giant aquarium, and able to see everything with crystal clarity through the window of his mask.

Very slowly, he followed Mick along the winding walls, between coral cliffs that grew farther and farther apart as they
20   approached the sea. At first the water was only two or three feet deep; then, quite abruptly, the bottom fell away almost vertically, and before Johnny realized what had happened, he was in water twenty feet deep. He had swum off the great plateau of the reef, and was heading for the open sea.

For a moment he was really frightened. He stopped swimming and marked time in the water, looking back over his shoulder to check that safety was only a few yards behind him. Then he looked ahead once more – ahead and downwards.

It was impossible to guess how far he could see into the
30   depths – a hundred feet, at least. He was looking down a long steep slope that led into a realm completely different from the

brightly lit, colourful pools which he had just left. From a world sparkling with sunlight, he was staring into a blue, mysterious gloom. And far down in that gloom, huge shapes were moving back and forth in a stately dance.

'What are they?' he whispered to his companion.

'Groupers,' said Mick. 'Watch.' Then, to Johnny's alarm, he slipped beneath the surface and arrowed down into the depths, as swiftly and gracefully as any fish.

40   He became smaller and smaller as he approached those moving shapes, and they seemed to grow in size by comparison. When he stopped, perhaps fifty feet down, he was floating just above them. He reached out, trying to touch one of the huge fish, but it gave a flick of its tail and eluded him.

Mick seemed in no hurry to return to the surface, but Johnny had taken at least a dozen breaths while he was watching the performance. At last, to the great relief of his audience, Mick began to swim slowly upward, waving goodbye to the groupers as he did so.

50   'How big were those fish?' asked Johnny when Mick had popped out of the water and recovered his breath.

'Oh, only eighty, a hundred pounds. You should see the really big ones up north. My grandfather hooked an eight-hundred-pounder off Cairns[1].'

'But you don't believe him,' grinned Johnny.

'But I do,' Mick grinned back. '*That* time he had a photograph to show it.'

As they swam back to the edge of the reef, Johnny glanced down once more into the blue depths, with their coral
60 boulders, their overhanging terraces, and the ponderous shapes swimming slowly among them. It was a world as alien as another planet, even though it was here on his own Earth. And it was a world that, because it was so utterly strange, filled him with curiosity and fear.

There was only one way of dealing with both these emotions. Sooner or later, he would have to follow Mick down that blue, mysterious slope.

ARTHUR C. CLARKE
Dolphin Island

[1] a town on the coast of Queensland, Australia

A *Comprehension*

1 How are you quickly made aware that this is a new experience for Johnny but not for Mick?

2 Why did Johnny quickly lose his fears on entering the pool?

3 (*a*) How could Johnny tell that he was swimming *towards* the sea?

   (*b*) How could he tell that he had reached the sea at the edge of the reef?

4 For what reasons was Johnny 'really frightened' (line 25) when he reached the sea?

5 How did his temporary fright affect his actions at that point?

6 What contrasts did he find between looking down into the pool and looking down into the sea?

7 Why was Johnny alarmed when Mick dived down towards the groupers?

8 What details suggest that Mick enjoyed his sea dive?

9 What made Johnny feel that he had made contact with 'a world as alien as another planet' (line 61) during this expedition?

10 (*a*) What were Johnny's main feelings after his experiences at the edge of the reef?

   (*b*) What effect did these feelings have on his future intentions?

B *Interpretation and criticism*

11 'Carved in the living rock' (line 4).

   (*a*) What imaginative impression of the ability of the water to wear away the rock is given by the use of the word 'carved'?

   (*b*) Why, in this particular case, is the rock described as 'living'?

12 'Johnny . . . lowered himself gingerly over the brittle coral' (line 11).

   (*a*) What sort of movement would you expect to see if someone moves 'gingerly'?

   (*b*) Why did Johnny lower himself 'gingerly'?

   (*c*) What qualities would you expect to find in something which is 'brittle'?

13 Why does the writer compare Johnny's underwater swimming with 'fish swimming in a giant aquarium' (line 16)?

14 Look up the meanings of the word 'realm' (line 31) in a good dictionary.

(a) What is the meaning of the word as it is used in the passage?

(b) Why is it a good word to use here?

(c) What use does the writer make of descriptive words to point the contrasts between the two 'realms'?

15 What qualities in Mick's movements through the water are suggested by the use of the word 'arrowed' (line 38)?

16 Why are the fish referred to as an 'audience' (line 47)?

17 What qualities of appearance – and, perhaps, movement – would you expect in '*ponderous* shapes' (line 60)?

18 The last sentence of the passage is also the last sentence of a chapter in the book from which the passage is taken. Why does it make an effective chapter ending? Which words particularly help to make it effective, and why?

19 (a) Which of the two characters in this passage is actually the main character in the story from which the passage is taken? How can you tell?

(b) How does the writer help *you* to identify with the main character in this passage?

20 (a) What do you find interesting about the scenes described in the passage?

(b) How does the writer help to make the scenes interesting to you?

(c) Why might the scenes not be as interesting without the presence of Johnny and Mick?

C *Ideas for writing*

21 Johnny's enjoyment of his expedition depended considerably on the fact that he was taken on it by Mick, an experienced diver. Write about an outing or expedition which you have enjoyed and on which you were able to be more adventurous because it was led by someone with plenty of experience of the places involved. Describe the events of the trip and write in detail about the most enjoyable or exciting moments.

22 Discuss some of the stories you have read where, as in this

passage, scenes in or near to water provide some of the most interesting episodes. Then, write a short story in which the climax is connected in some way with water, and in which the action either takes place in or on water or close to water.

D Suggestions for reading

This passage comes from Arthur C. Clarke's science fiction novel *Dolphin Island*, set on a South Pacific island off the Great Barrier Reef in the twenty-first century. It is an unusual story about man's attempts to establish working relationships with dolphins and to control the killing instincts of creatures such as killer whales by implanting electrical impulses in their brains. Readers of *Dolphin Island* are given a fascinating insight into these experiments through the presence of Johnny at Professor Kazan's experimental station on Dolphin Island. Johnny has been shipwrecked and his packing-case raft has been towed to safety at the island by a group of dolphins!

Dolphin Island is available as a Piccolo Science Fiction paperback. Other science fiction stories by Arthur C. Clarke in paperback include *Islands in the Sky* and *Of Time and the Stars*, both available in Puffins.

You can find more suggestions for science fiction reading on page 54.

3
Death's drummer boy

Cortachy Castle is an ancient Scottish fortress in the wilds of
Angus, the home of the Ogilvies, and family seat of the Earls of
Airlie. For many years a ghost has haunted the household, a
drummer whose playing foretells the coming of a death in the
family.

Many years ago, one of the Earls had a young drummer
among his servants, a strong young man, handsome and
charming and full of fun. Women could not resist him, and he
enjoyed their attentions. It may be that even the Earl's wife lost
10 her heart to the dashing young fellow. Whatever the cause, the
Earl was very jealous. Many a time he hotly warned the servant
of his behaviour with the women of the house. And once, in a
fit of jealous rage, the Earl threatened the drummer's life.
There followed a violent quarrel between master and servant,
and the drummer told the Earl that if he ever carried out his
threat, he, the drummer, would haunt the Ogilvies for ever
afterwards.

The Earl cannot have believed him. For one night he and
some of his men trapped the drummer in an upstairs room.
20 They tied the young man's hands and feet, thrust his drum
over his head, and threw him out of the window onto the stone
paving below. The drummer died instantly.

Since that time, whenever a member of the Ogilvie family is
near death – whether they know it or not – a ghostly drum is
heard beating a tattoo in the castle or somewhere nearby on
the estate.

Many people have heard that deathly warning. In 1844 a
young lady, a Miss Dalrymple, was visiting Cortachy. She was
dressing for dinner on the night of her arrival when she heard
30 coming from just below her window the faint sound of a drum.
There was a hollowness, an unearthly quality in the sound that

11

caught Miss Dalrymple's attention. The beating got louder. She looked out of the window to find out who was playing, but saw no one.

During dinner, Miss Dalrymple asked Lord Airlie during a pause in the conversation, 'My Lord, who is your drummer?'

The Earl turned pale and stopped eating. Lady Airlie also seemed upset. Everyone at the table sat in silent embarrassment. Miss Dalrymple could see that somehow she had said the
40 wrong thing, and let the topic go by. After dinner, however, she took a younger member of the family aside and asked again about the drummer.

'What!' he said. 'Have you never heard of the drummer boy?'

'Never,' said Miss Dalrymple. 'Who is he?'

'Why,' said the young Ogilvie, 'he is a ghost who goes about the house playing his drum whenever there is to be a death in the family. The last time he was heard was shortly before the death of the Earl's first wife. That is why he turned so pale just now. It is a very unpleasant subject in this family, I assure you.'
50 Now it was Miss Dalrymple who felt upset. More than this, the idea of a ghost drumming his way round the castle frightened her somewhat. And when she heard him drumming again next day, she invented an excuse to leave Cortachy and return home.

Nearly six months later news came that Lady Airlie, the Earl's second wife, had died while on a trip to Brighton. By her side was a note saying she had known from the time Miss Dalrymple mentioned the drummer that he was tattooing her own death warning.
60 Five years later, on the evening of August 19th, 1849, a young Englishman was riding across the Forfarshire moors on his way to a shooting party on the Cortachy estate. It was already dark when the Englishman came in sight of the lighted windows of the shooting lodge. Just then, he heard the faint swelling sound of a band accompanied by a drum. The music seemed to be coming from a ridge of ground between the Englishman and the house. The rider reined in his horse and listened. The music grew louder, and the young man could not help feeling there was something eerie, unnatural about the
70 sound. In a few moments, to his great relief, the music died away.

The Englishman rode on. It was when he arrived at the

shooting lodge that he learned for the first time that his friend
and host, the Earl's eldest son, had been called to London
urgently. The Earl was dangerously ill. The following day, he
died. The Englishman's friend succeeded as the tenth Earl of
Cortachy Castle. But like all the Ogilvies, he lived in dread of
hearing the ghostly drummer beat out his mortal music.

AIDAN CHAMBERS
Haunted Houses

A *Comprehension*

1 What information in the passage suggests that earlier
   generations of the Earls of Airlie had to make their own ar-
   rangements to defend their family?
2 What do you learn from this passage about the surroundings of Cortachy Castle?
3 What were the drummer's likeable qualities when he was
   alive?
4 Why was the drummer particularly unwise in his behaviour
   during the period immediately before his death?
5 What do we learn about the character of the Earl responsible for the drummer's murder?
6 'For one night he and some of his men trapped the drummer in an upstairs room' (line 18).
   (*a*) What does this information suggest about the Earl's
   suspicions and intentions regarding the drummer?
   (*b*) How might the drummer have come to be 'trapped . . .
   in an upstairs room'?
7 How and why did Miss Dalrymple cause embarrassment to
   the Airlie family at Cortachy?
8 Why did Miss Dalrymple decide to go home early from the
   castle?
9 What proof is there in the passage that a member of the
   Ogilvie family can sometimes sense when the drummer is
   foretelling his or her death?
10 What evidence is there in the passage that the sounds of
   the ghostly drummer possess special qualities to attract the
   attention of the listener?

B *Interpretation and criticism*

11 Sometimes words are used deliberately to fire the reader's imagination. What pictures do the words 'fortress' and 'wilds' (line 1) conjure up in your mind at the beginning of this story?

12 What qualities would you expect to find in a *'dashing young fellow'* (line 10)?

13 Look up the meaning of the word 'rage' (line 13) in a good dictionary. Why does the writer rightly use it here instead of a word such as 'anger' or 'temper'?

14 (*a*) Look up the derivation and the meanings of the word 'tattoo' (line 25) in a good dictionary.
(*b*) Why, do you think, did the ghostly drummer make a point of 'beating a *tattoo*' (line 25)?

15 In what ways does the introduction of conversation during the account of Miss Dalrymple's visit to Cortachy help to make the passage more dramatic at that point?

16 Explore the various meanings of the word 'lodge' in a good dictionary.
(*a*) What is a 'shooting lodge' (line 64)?
(*b*) Why would a shooting lodge be necessary on the Cortachy estate, do you think?

17 What sorts of sounds or happenings do you associate with the use of the word 'eerie' (line 69)?

18 'He lived in dread of hearing the ghostly drummer beat out his mortal music' (line 77).
(*a*) Why does the writer deliberately use the word 'dread' rather than the word 'fear'?
(*b*) Look up the meaning of the word 'mortal' in a good dictionary and then explain why the music is described as being 'mortal'.

19 The title of this passage is that given by the writer Aidan Chambers. Why is it an effective title, do you think?

20 (*a*) In what ways does the writer make sure that this story is made as creepy as possible for his readers?
(*b*) How does the *setting* of the story help to provide extra food for the imagination?

21 Both the incidents concerning the ghostly drummer took place during the nineteenth century. Try to discover, from books about ghosts and the supernatural in either your

school library or local public library, whether such incidents are still taking place in the twentieth century. Have the Ogilvies heard the drummer recently? Do other families living in large houses, or on large estates, have similar hauntings?

C *Ideas for writing*

22 What kinds of places seem to attract ghosts or other supernatural happenings? Discuss some typical settings for eerie stories. Take the setting which you think is a particularly suitable one – a graveyard, a lonely wood, a ruined church, for example – and write your own tale of the supernatural, a tale leading to a frightening climax in your chosen setting.

23 Today it is possible to find furnished holiday accommodation in all sorts of unusual buildings in remote areas, buildings which include, for instance, castles, country houses, windmills, water towers and fishermen's cottages. Imagine going on holiday with your family to one such building. The locals tell you on your arrival that strange things happen where you are staying. Needless to say you don't believe them, until one night . . . .. Write the story of your holiday adventure.

D *Suggestions for reading*

This passage comes from a book written by Aidan Chambers, *Haunted Houses*. All the stories in the book are about real houses which are genuinely believed to be haunted, and you can visit some of them. If you enjoyed this tale, then the titles of others in the collection will attract you: 'The Nameless Horror of Berkeley Square' and 'The Ghostly Skulls of Calgarth Hall', for instance. The book has been published as a Piccolo Original paperback by Pan Books Ltd, and there is also a sequel, *More Haunted Houses*, and a number of collections of *Monster Books*, as well as two books by Peter Haining, *The Restless Bones and Other True Mysteries*, and *The Monster Trap and Other True Mysteries*. Aidan Chambers has also written *Great Ghosts of the World* and *Great British Ghosts* for Piccolo paperbacks.

4
Susan and
the village children

The village children laughed and pointed at her.

'What's your name?' they shouted.

'Susanna Catherine Mary Garland,' replied Susan, with her dark eyes wide and startled.

'What's your father?' they sang, swaying and swinging in a row, and pushing against her.

'I don't know,' said Susan, hesitating. It was the first time she had thought of this. In her little world there were no trades.

10 'Where do you come from?' they jeered, louder and louder, as they rocked with laughter at her simplicity.

Susan was on safe ground now. Had she not written it on the milk tickets each morning?

'From Windystone Hall, near Mellow,' she replied with a shy pride, as she thought of her domain[1], the wide fields and woods, the rambling house and buildings, and compared it with the tiny rose-filled gardens and thatched cottages of the village.

'Windy stone, rain stone, who went down the lane alone?'
20 mocked a wit, and the children shook back their hair and yelled with glee.

'Aye. What a figure of fun. Where did you get that frock?' they gibed.

She had loathed her dress, but now she held it tightly with one hand. It came from her own home, and was part of her. She had been called 'a figure of fun'. She stood with her back against the wall and a crowd of jeering girls jostled her. One pulled her hair with a mischievous tug, one opened her satchel and looked at her sandwiches, and one, the most shameless,

[1] estate, home territory

16

30 put her tongue out at her. A little boy her own age ran up
rudely and kissed her. He rushed away screaming with laughter, and Susan took out her handkerchief and rubbed her
cheek as the cries and jibes rose higher. She stood like a
frightened rabbit, her face white, her eyes big with horror.
'Mother,' she whispered to her heart, and the school bell rang.

ALISON UTTLEY
The Country Child

A Comprehension

1 Why did the village children ask Susan so many questions?
2 (a) What do you think Susan's father did for a living?
   (b) What information in the passage suggests this?
3 Why, then, did Susan say 'I don't know', when the children
asked 'What's your father?' (line 5)?
4 (a) Why did Susan feel 'on safe ground' (line 12) when asked where she came from?
   (b) Why did she have a feeling of 'shy pride' (line 14) when
she told the children where she lived?
5 Why might the fact that Susan lived at Windystone Hall
have made the children tease her more than they might
have teased a *village* girl coming to school for the first
time?
6 Try to explain in your own words the main differences between the sort of surroundings in which Susan lived and
those in which the village children lived.
7 Why do you think Susan was particularly upset when the
children made fun of her dress?
8 (a) At what time of day do you think that all this happened?
   (b) Where did it happen?
9 Why, in your opinion, did Susan whisper the word
'Mother' (line 35) as the children's teasing got worse and
worse?
10 What might have happened next, if the bell hadn't rung?
11 After studying the passage, what do you think were the
main reasons for the village children's teasing and making
fun of Susan?

B *Interpretation and criticism*

12 Why were Susan's eyes 'wide and startled' (line 4) when the children started to laugh and to ask questions?

13 'In her little world there were no trades' (line 8). What and where was Susan's 'little world' before she started school?

14 The children 'jeered' at Susan (line 10).
(*a*) What is 'jeering' and when do people 'jeer'?
(*b*) How does the *sound* of the word help to suggest its meaning?
(*c*) Which other words used in the passage have similar meanings to the word 'jeered'?

15 What do you think the milk tickets mentioned on line 13 might have been used for?

16 Susan's house is described as 'rambling' (line 16). What would you imagine a rambling house to look like inside, and, perhaps, outside?

17 'She had *loathed* her dress' (line 24).
(*a*) What does the word 'loathed' suggest about her feelings for the dress in the past?
(*b*) At this moment why does Susan feel differently about the dress?

18 The girls 'jostled' Susan (line 27).
Can you describe the actions involved when you are 'jostled'?

19 (*a*) Would the children have behaved as unpleasantly towards Susan if they hadn't been together in a bunch?
(*b*) Can you explain why?
(*c*) Can you think of any other kinds of occasions when people behave more unpleasantly as members of a crowd than they would do as individuals?

20 'She stood like a frightened rabbit' (line 34).
Why is the comparison of Susan with a frightened rabbit a good choice of comparison here?

C *Ideas for writing*

21 Going to school for the first time, or going to a new school, can be a worrying experience, both during the days beforehand and on the day when you arrive and have to

find your way round a strange building and to encounter new sets of class mates and teachers for the first time. Write about your memories of your first day at a new school, your first school, perhaps, or, later, your first day at a bigger school such as a middle school or a comprehensive school.

22 Susan suffered teasing of a most unpleasant kind on her first morning at school. What kinds of teasing can be particularly unpleasant and even cruel, and on what sorts of occasions do you encounter them?

Can teasing sometimes be actually enjoyable? Under what circumstances can it be so? Try to remember some of the occasions when you have either gained pleasure or suffered unhappiness from being teased, and write about these occasions.

D Suggestions for reading

This passage comes from Alison Uttley's story *A Country Child*. Susan is the country child and this book describes her childhood, her journeys to and from school through the frightening Dark Wood, her home at the old farmhouse, Windystone Hall, and her life at home. We are taken back to the days of the horse and trap, of driving home with carriage lamps lit, of walking home with the aid of a lantern. It is a quiet, imaginative book, and is available as a Puffin paperback.

An interesting contrast between Susan's life in the English countryside almost a century ago and the life of an American girl who was a member of a pioneering family travelling across the American mid-west in the nineteenth century can be discovered if you read the true stories about Laura in the novels by Laura Ingalls Wilder. The passage entitled 'The Long Rifle' on pages 34 to 36 comes from one of these novels and you can find details of these on page 38. Laura's first day at school is described in chapter twenty of *On the Banks of Plum Creek*, a Puffin paperback. One of Leslie Thomas's boyhood experiences of his first days at a Barnardo Home is described in the passage 'Good old Monkey!' on pages 20 to 21, and on page 23 you can obtain details of the book from which it is taken, *This Time Next Week*.

5
Good old Monkey!

The day after I arrived at the Kingston home from Woodford I was nicknamed. They called me Monkey. I went into the dormitory on the second night and there was a reception committee sitting on the beds. They wouldn't let me go past so I stood, trembling inside, looking at them.

As boys go they looked villainous enough. Jerseys, blue and grey, patched all over, trousers embroidered in the same way, socks around ankles and bursting shoes.

"lo Monkey,' said one kid standing in my way.

10   'Trying to be funny?' I said.

'Yeah, Monkey,' he grinned. 'Let's see you swing on the beams.'

The others all laughed and I knew I was going to have a fight.

'What do they call you, then?' I said to the spokesman. 'Is it Ape? Or Chimp?'

He hit me on the side of the head with a sharp, stony fist. I thought he'd knocked my eye out of its socket. I went straight over the iron bedrail and landed in the hard valley between two

20 beds. My head was screaming and I could hear them all roaring around and above me. I heard someone shrieking 'A fight! The new kid's 'aving a fight!' From the next dormitory came a deluge of booted onlookers.

I knew I'd have to get up and I knew just as certainly that he would put me on my back again. Having caught me with the sudden swing, he now pranced about at the ends of the beds between which I lay, shadow boxing and yelling to me to rise and fight him. At that moment I couldn't even focus him too well, but I thought he was no bigger than me. It was just that

30 he'd hit me first.

'Come on out, Monkey,' he yelled. 'Let's see your monkey face.'

20

My leg must have been sticking out because he got hold of it and pulled me out. They were leaping on the beds, and shouting and laughing. It was like being in a cave with them all calling down at me.

The fighter got hold of my foot again. My shoe came off and he staggered back against one of the beds. When he came back I was up to meet him. I never could fight. But I was bristling
40 with tears and temper. I ran at him and felt the top of my head crunch his nose. He swore in short words. Now I was there I hit him with both fists, my bony elbows and caught him a cruel thrust with my pointed knee.

He was on the ground and I was on him, my angry fingers on his hair, banging his head against the ground. His nose was discharging like a red river. In the end they pulled me off and in the true manner of boys carried me away in noisy glory while they left him to bleed.

I might have won my fight but I had not gained my point.
50 Even in the flush of victory they were calling: 'He's won! Monkey's won! Good old Monkey! Good old Monkey!'

LESLIE THOMAS
This Time Next Week

A Comprehension

1 How was it clear to the writer that he faced trouble when he entered the dormitory on the second night?
2 Why did the reactions of the group of boys to their 'spokesman' (line 15) make the writer convinced that he was going to have a fight?
3 What happened to make the fight actually start?
4 What evidence is there that the boys *wanted* to see this fight?
5 What were the writer's main disadvantages in the fight, to begin with?
6 What evidence is there that the boys had indeed chosen the right '*spokesman*' for their purpose?
7 At what point did the 'spokesman' lose his advantage?
8 How did the writer's state of mind help him to win the fight?

9 (a) How did the boys behave towards the writer once he had made his opponent's nose bleed?

(b) Why did they behave like this, do you think?

(c) Why did they leave their spokesman to bleed?

10 Why was the writer not entirely satisfied with the final outcome?

11 In what ways might the writer's victory in the fight have changed things for him afterwards?

B Interpretation and criticism

12 (a) What are 'nicknames' (line 2)?

(b) When are nicknames most often used?

(c) When can they be used unkindly?

13 (a) With what kinds of occasion would you *usually* associate a 'reception committee' (line 3)?

(b) What is the purpose of *this* 'reception committee'?

14 Why is the fist of the boy who hit the writer described as 'stony' (line 17)?

15 Why does the writer describe the space between the two beds as 'the hard valley' (line 19)?

16 What would the boy look like and how would he move as he '*pranced* about at the end of the beds . . .' (line 26)?

17 (a) What is 'shadow boxing' (line 27)?

(b) Why did the boy do some shadow boxing, do you think?

18 'I was bristling with tears and temper' (line 39).

(a) Why does the writer use the word 'bristling' here?

(b) What else, other than the actual blows, might have produced the writer's tears?

19 What is Leslie Thomas suggesting about the typical behaviour of boys after a fight when he writes that '*in the true manner of boys*' they 'carried me away in *noisy glory...*' (line 47)?

20 (a) In what ways is the behaviour of the boys towards the writer typical of that of a group of boys towards newcomers?

(b) Why do boys behave in this way?

21 Look again at the passage 'Susan and the village children' on pages 16 to 17 and compare it with this passage.

(a) In what ways do the passages reflect the age differences of the younger Susan and the older Leslie?

(*b*) How do Susan and Leslie react to the pressures placed on them and how does this reflect their different characters and backgrounds? (Leslie's parents had both died and he had not had an easy childhood.)

(*c*) What do both passages perhaps suggest about the different ways in which individual children react to being pressured or teased by members of a hostile group?

C *Ideas for writing*

22 Write a story entitled 'The Nickname' which centres on the character who is given the nickname and in which the climax is connected with the use of the nickname. Remember that some nicknames are given out of a sense of dislike of a person whilst others can be regarded as compliments. The climax of your story will really depend on *why* your character has been given his or her nickname.

23 Why do newcomers often need help and sympathy and why are they sometimes not given it, and even resented? Discuss the difficulties faced by newcomers in various situations and then write a story, true or imaginary, about the experiences of a newcomer who was either helped and welcomed or was treated unkindly.

D *Suggestions for reading*

Leslie Thomas's book, *This Time Next Week*, from which this passage is taken, is the story of his own childhood and youth spent as a 'Barnardo Boy' following the death of both his parents. It contains some extremely funny episodes – the one involving the goats, for instance – but it is also a clear, honest account of life in a Home, often moving because it is so free of self-pity and so full of a determination to find happiness in life as an orphan. It is published as a Pan paperback.

During the Second World War, which is the time of Leslie Thomas's book, many children had to go and live away from their parents when their homes were in danger from bombing. These children were known as 'evacuees' and a very good story about the strangeness of the new lives frequently encountered by these evacuees is Nina Bawden's fine book *Carrie's War*, available as a Puffin paperback.

An interesting book about what it was like to be a girl orphan is Janet Hitchman's *King of the Barbareens*, an autobiographical account of life in the Barkingside Village Home and with foster parents. It is available as a Penguin Peacock paperback.

6
A visit to The Shambles

Poll knew quite well why her mother disliked Annie Dowsett because she liked her for just the same reason. Annie was rough, she wore old clothes all the time, she fought with boys and was ready for anything. She even agreed to accompany Poll into the slummy part of the Town, called The Shambles, a tightly packed jumble of narrow streets and old houses that Aunt Sarah said no nicely brought up girl would walk through, even in daylight, and certainly not after dark. 'I'd be scared,' Lily said with a shudder, and so, naturally, Poll wanted to go
10 there.

She and Annie went into The Shambles the last day of the Easter Term, after school. Poll was nervous at first, not knowing what to expect, and then disappointed to find nothing really alarming, only a rather dirty place where vegetable rubbish squelched underfoot and women stood on their doorsteps and gossiped while their babies played around their feet.

Poll thought she had never seen so many babies, fat ones and thin ones, pale ones and rosy ones, crawling in the dirt, clinging to their mothers' skirts, or sitting, grubby and grumbling,
20 in rickety prams. One baby stopped crying and smiled at her when she picked up his rattle from the ground where he'd thrown it. His fat cheeks were solid and shiny. Poll said to his mother, 'Look, he likes me. Can I take him for a walk, do you think?'

The woman looked at Poll without answering. She was tall and big in the chest with a dark, heavy face and hard glistening eyes, like dark glass. When she started to laugh, throwing her head back, Poll saw that she had a lot of teeth missing and that one of those that were left was long and sharp, like a spike, or a
30 fang. She stared, fascinated, and then realised that the woman was laughing at *her*. As she backed away, the woman on the

25

next doorstep began laughing too, and the next woman, and
the next, until the cruel, raucous noise seemed to fill the whole
street and press on her ear-drums like thunder. Annie grabbed
at her hand. 'Come on,' she said urgently, '*run . . .*'

They ran, mud splashing their legs – and worse things than
mud, Poll thought, wrinkling her nose – through mean,
twisting alleys, past dark, open-doored hovels and staring slat-
ternly[1] women, to the safety of the wide Market Square. They
40 filled their lungs with clean air and looked at each other, Poll
sheepishly, Annie astonished. 'Why ever d'you want to speak to
her for? Bit daft, warn't it?'

'I don't know.' Poll felt sick with shame. That horrible, jeering laughter still rang in her head.

'Lucky she warn't drunk, or she might've clobbered you one
for your cheek,' Annie said.

'I only asked to take her baby out, didn't I? That wasn't
rude!'

'Bit queer-like, though. I spec' she thought you was mental.'
50 'Don't see why. I like playing with babies. And we haven't
any at home, in our family.'

Annie shrugged. 'If you want babies, you c'n come to my
house and welcome, any time you've a mind to.'

'Thank you,' Poll said. 'I'd like to some time. I'll ask my
mother.' She hoped it didn't show in her face that she knew
Mother would never give her permission.

NINA BAWDEN
The Peppermint Pig

A Comprehension

1 What evidence is there in the first paragraph that Annie
was 'ready for anything' (line 4)?

2 Why did her sister Lily's statement 'I'd be scared' (line 8)
make Poll even more keen to visit The Shambles, do you
think?

3 How and why did Poll's feelings change soon after she
entered The Shambles?

[1] untidy and slovenly

4 'Look, he likes me. Can I take him for a walk, do you think?' (line 23).
   For what reasons other than the fact that the baby seemed to 'like' Poll might she have asked the mother if she could take it for a walk?

5 What made first the mother and then the other women laugh?

6 (a) Why did Poll stare at the mother?
   (b) Why did she stop staring and start backing away from her?

7 Why did Annie tell Poll to run?

8 'They filled their lungs with clean air . . .' (line 39).
   Why were they unable to do this until they reached the Market Square?

9 What made Poll feel 'sick with shame' (line 43)?

10 Explain in your own words why Annie thought Poll had been silly to talk to the mother and to ask to take her baby out.

11 (a) Why, particularly, did Annie give an open invitation to Poll to visit her house?
   (b) Why would Poll's mother 'never give her permission' (line 56) for Poll to visit Annie's house?

B Interpretation and criticism

12 What do the words 'tightly packed jumble' (line 6) suggest about the layout of streets and houses in The Shambles?

13 (a) What does Aunt Sarah mean when she speaks of a girl who is 'nicely brought up' (line 7)?
   (b) To Aunt Sarah, what kind of girl might *not* be 'nicely brought up'?

14 (a) When do people 'shudder' (line 9)?
   (b) What sort of movements are involved in 'shuddering'?

15 'Vegetable rubbish *squelched* underfoot' (line 14).
   (a) What does the word 'squelched' tell you about conditions underfoot?
   (b) Why is 'squelched' such a good word to describe both the action and the *sound* of the action?

16 What do you think the babies' prams would have looked like if the writer describes them as 'rickety' (line 20)?

17 How does the writer's choice of comparisons when describ-

ing the eyes and the teeth of the baby's mother help to emphasise her rather frightening appearance?

18 What are the special qualities of a *'raucous* noise' (line 33)?

19 What sort of conditions would you expect to find in a house which is described as a 'hovel' (line 38)?

20 Why did Poll look 'sheepishly' (line 41) at Annie once they reached the Market Square?

21 What differences are there between the ways in which Poll and Annie speak?

22 What differences between the family backgrounds of Poll and Annie are revealed or hinted at in this passage, particularly in the attitudes of Poll's mother towards Annie?

23 (a) What evidence is there in the passage that the people who live in The Shambles are looked down on by people elsewhere in the town?

   (b) What evidence is there to suggest that the people in The Shambles probably stick closely together as a result?

C Ideas for writing

24 Most of you will have had the experience of taking a baby out in its pram or the experience of looking after a baby for some time. Often, the unexpected happens in the course of these experiences. The baby doesn't want to go to sleep, or it is teething and in an evil frame of mind, or it makes a dreadful mess of itself when you try to feed it, or you get into a terrible tangle trying to dress it or change its nappy. Write a story, real or imaginary, comic or serious, or both, entitled 'Looking after Baby'.

25 Look carefully at the description of the baby's mother (lines 25 to 30). Then, use this description as the starting point for a story in which you meet her and find that underneath her rather frightening appearance and manner, she is actually kind and warm-hearted.

D Suggestions for reading

When Poll's father loses his job in London and sets off for America to seek his fortune, Poll and her family go off to live with her mother's sister in Norfolk. There, life is made fun for them when mother buys a 'little runt of a peppermint pig' from the milk man for a shilling, and the pig, Johnnie, is brought up in the house as a pet. You can read about the adventures of Poll, and the pig, in Nina Bawden's pleasant family tale, *The Peppermint Pig*, from which this passage is taken. It is available as a Puffin paperback.

Other stories by Nina Bawden, all published as Puffins, include *Carrie's War, A Handful of Thieves, On the Run, Runaway Summer, Squib*, and *The Witch's Daughter*. If you enjoy the Norfolk setting of *The Peppermint Pig* you might try another story set in Norfolk, Joan Robinson's *When Marnie Was There*, the tale of Anna, a lonely foster-child, who goes to stay in Norfolk and there, at an old house by a creek, meets the mysterious Marnie. Published by Collins, *When Marnie Was There* has appeared as an Armada Lion paperback.

For an exciting adventure story set in the lonely Fen Country adjoining Norfolk, try Stephen Chance's *Septimus and the Danedyke Mystery*. The passage 'Miss Crowle's strange encounter' on pages 74 to 77 comes from this book and you can find more details in the 'Suggestions for reading ' on page 80.

7
The bonfire

All the chairs and sofas were somehow erected into a pyre, and
the hideous Guy that had done such a good begging job was
hoisted to the very top and posed there on a chair with three
legs. A rocket was stuck in the Guy's arms and a sparkler on his
head. From somewhere Val conjured up a tin of paraffin, and
he struck the first match, while the others shoved and grabbed
trying to get at the match box.

    At one moment, the bomb site had been a dark, bare area
with a few shadowy figures lugging heavy objects, and then –
10 as the match tickled up the paraffin, fire leapt out. In a moment the whole place was a wild inferno of crackling flames,
jumping squibs, shooting rockets, bouncing bangers and
whizzers. Dozens of demonic figures yelled and ran and leapt
about, for in a few seconds the children had multiplied into
hundreds.

    Up, up, shot the flames, sending great sprays and showers of
sparks into the night. All the old chairs, full of worm, beetle,
and dry horse hair, caught like tinder and made a glowing core
to the fire. Whizzers and bangers were now going off all over
20 the place, exploding like jumping jacks in the very middle of
the crowd, and starting yells of dismay and small fights.
Screaming girls ran away and were pursued. All the windows in
the houses around the bomb site had shot up, and their in-
habitants were yelling protests and complaints, but not one of
the children listened. Some of the adults saw the fun of the
fire, but the duller ones, who were only greedy for their rights
as citizens, rang up the police, the fire brigade, the Vicar or
anyone else they fancied.

    Val and his gang were in their glory. For weeks they had
30 been planning this night, counting their pennies and dreaming
of rockets. Their faces and hands were by now, if possible,

blacker than usual. As the rockets went up and broke into a
myriad of coloured stars, red, green and orange, their hearts
seemed to soar too and explode in sparks of pleasure.
Yet hardly had the fire attained its full height, before the
children heard the ringing of the engines' bells. Huge, red
machines were rushing from every direction towards the bomb
site.
'They're coming!' yelled Val. 'Look out, chaps, the brigade's
40 here.' Close behind the brigade were the black police cars.

ELIZABETH STUCLEY
Magnolia Buildings

A Comprehension

1 What exactly is a 'Guy' and why is it so called?
2 Why was the Guy only placed on top of the pile of chairs
and sofas just before the bonfire was lit?
3 Why, probably, were old chairs and sofas the main fuel for
the fire?
4 What clear evidence is there in the passage that Val was
the leader of the gang?
5 What sort of 'heavy objects' do you think the 'shadowy
figures' were 'lugging' (line 9)?
6 Why, do you think, did the bonfire burn so well?
7 (a) What sort of fireworks did the children seem to prefer?
(b) Why, perhaps?
8 (a) What started the complaints from some of the adults?
(b) Why did they complain?
(c) Why did some adults *not* complain?
9 (a) Which moment seemed to be the high spot of the evening for Val and his gang?
(b) What evidence is there that this was a moment they
had been looking forward to for a long time?

B Interpretation and criticism

10 Look up the word 'pyre' (line 1) in a good dictionary.
Why does the writer describe the heap of chairs and sofas
as a 'pyre'?

11 Why, perhaps, is the Guy described as being 'hideous' (line 2)?

12 If the Guy was 'hoisted' (line 3) what does this suggest about the *size* of the bonfire?

13 'A few shadowy figures lugging heavy objects' (line 9).
(*a*) Why are the figures described as being 'shadowy' at this moment?
(*b*) What does the word 'lugging' suggest about the way the children moved these objects?

14 A description full of sound becomes more exciting when a writer uses words which actually seem to make the sounds described. Pick out some of the sound words in the second and third paragraphs of this passage and say why they help to convey the sounds of the bonfire, the fireworks and the people to you.

15 Why does the writer repeat the word 'up' in her statement 'Up, up shot the flames...' (line 16)?

16 Why do writers often use the word 'showers', when describing a fire, in the phrase 'showers of sparks' (line 16)?

17 Windows 'shot up' in nearby houses (line 23).
What do the words 'shot up' suggest about the feelings of the people living in these houses?

18 Look up the words 'inferno' (line 11) and 'demonic' (line 13) in a good dictionary. Having done so, can you work out
(*a*) why the word 'inferno' is often used in describing a big fire?
(*b*) why the writer uses the word 'demonic' to describe the yelling and leaping figures by the fire?

19 What is meant by the statement 'Val and his gang *were in their glory*' (line 29)?

20 (*a*) After the Second World War there were many 'bomb sites' in British towns and cities. Try to find out what 'bomb sites' were.
(*b*) Why were they often good places to have bonfires?

21 (*a*) What evidence is there in the passage that the writer is sympathetic towards the children and that she appreciates why they enjoyed the bonfire and the fireworks?
(*b*) Is there any suggestion that the writer was not very sympathetic towards the adults who sent for the fire brigade and the police?

C *Ideas for writing*

22 Exciting things *can* happen to ordinary children in ordinary situations in ordinary surroundings. Val and his friends had an exciting bonfire night, with an extra adventure provided by the arrival of the fire brigade. Adventure need not involve larger-than-life heroes or villains or hair-raising chases in foreign countries. Prove that adventure can lie on your own doorstep by telling the story of an incident in *your* life which *you* have found exciting. You might find the title 'Quite An Adventure' helpful.

23 Why do both children and adults enjoy watching bonfires, particularly at night? Is the enjoyment in some way connected with the warmth and protection and defence which fire provided for primitive man living in the wilds thousands of years ago? Write a description or a story – real or imaginary – about your own experiences of making a bonfire and of watching it burn up and eventually die down so that only the glowing embers are left. (The bonfire in your account needn't necessarily be connected with Guy Fawkes night.)

D *Suggestions for reading*

This passage is taken from Elizabeth Stucley's story of children in a London suburb, *Magnolia Buildings*. It is a story which finds adventure and entertainment amongst ordinary everyday surroundings. It is available in a Puffin paperback.

John Rowe Townsend has written a number of lively stories about children living in a Northern town. Two of the most popular are *Gumble's Yard* and its sequel *Hell's Edge*; both are obtainable in Puffin paperbacks. The inner city area of Liverpool is the setting for Sylvia Sherry's sensitive and entertaining story of Liverpool teenagers, *A Pair of Jesus Boots*, also available in Puffin paperbacks.

The streets of Manchester provide the starting point for Alan Garner's unusual and sometimes frightening tale of magic and the supernatural, *Elidor*, published by Collins.

8
The long rifle

Every evening before he began to tell stories, Pa made the bullets for his next day's hunting.

Laura and Mary helped him. They brought the big, long-handled spoon, and the box full of bits of lead, and the bullet-mould. Then while he squatted on the hearth and made the bullets, they sat one on each side of him, and watched.

First he melted the bits of lead in the big spoon held in the coals. When the lead was melted, he poured it carefully from the spoon into the little hole in the bullet-mould. He waited a
10 minute, then he opened the mould, and out dropped a bright new bullet on to the hearth.

The bullet was too hot to touch, but it shone so temptingly that Laura or Mary could not help touching it. Then they burned their fingers. But they did not say anything, because Pa had told them never to touch a new bullet. If they burned their fingers, that was their own fault; they should have minded him. So they put their fingers in their mouths to cool them, and watched Pa make more bullets.

There would be a shining pile of them on the hearth before
20 Pa stopped. He let them cool, then with his jack-knife he trimmed off the little lumps left by the hole in the mould. He gathered up the tiny shavings of lead and saved them carefully, to melt again the next time he made bullets.

The finished bullets he put into his bullet pouch. This was a little bag which Ma had made beautifully of buck-skin, from a buck Pa had shot.

After the bullets were made, Pa would take his gun down from the wall and clean it. Out in the snowy woods all day, it might have gathered a little dampness, and the inside of the
30 barrel was sure to be dirty from powder smoke.

So Pa would take the ramrod from its place under the gun

barrel, and fasten a piece of clean cloth on its end. He stood the butt of the gun in a pan on the hearth and poured boiling water from the tea kettle into the gun barrel. Then quickly he dropped the ramrod in and rubbed it up and down, up and down, while the hot water blackened with powder smoke spurted out through the little hole on which the cap was placed when the gun was loaded.

40 Pa kept pouring in more water and washing the gun barrel with the cloth on the ramrod until the water ran out clear. Then the gun was clean. The water must always be boiling, so that the heated steel would dry instantly.

Then Pa put a clean greased rag on the ramrod, and while the gun barrel was still hot he greased it well on the inside. With another clean, greased cloth he rubbed it all over, outside, until every bit of it was oiled and sleek. After that he rubbed and polished the gunstock until the wood of it was bright and shining, too.

50 Now he was ready to load the gun again, and Laura and Mary must help him. Standing straight and tall, holding the long gun upright on its butt, while Laura and Mary stood on either side of him, Pa said:

'You watch me, now, and tell me if I make a mistake.'

So they watched very carefully, but he never made a mistake.

Laura handed him the smooth, polished cow-horn full of gunpowder. The top of the horn was a little metal cap. Pa filled this cap full of the gunpowder and poured the powder down the barrel of the gun. Then he shook the gun a little, and tap-
60 ped the barrel, to be sure that all the powder was together in the bottom.

'Where's my patch box?' he asked then, and Mary gave him the little tin box full of little pieces of greased cloth. Pa laid one of these bits of greasy cloth over the muzzle of the gun, put one of the shiny new bullets on it, and with the ramrod he pushed the bullet and the cloth down the gun barrel.

Then he pounded them tightly against the powder. When he hit them with the ramrod, the ramrod bounced up in the gun barrel, and Pa caught it and thrust it down again. He did this
70 for a long time.

Next he put the ramrod back in its place against the gun barrel. Then taking a box of caps from his pocket, he raised the hammer of the gun and slipped one of the little bright caps over the hollow pin that was under the hammer.

He let the hammer down, slowly and carefully. If it came down quickly – bang! – the gun would go off.

Now the gun was loaded, and Pa laid it on its hooks over the door.

When Pa was at home the gun always lay across those two wooden hooks above the door. Pa had whittled the hooks out of a green stick with his knife, and had driven their straight ends deep into holes in the log. The hooked ends curved upward and held the gun securely.

The gun was always loaded, and always above the door so that Pa could get it quickly and easily, any time he needed a gun.

LAURA INGALLS WILDER
Little House in the Big Woods

A *Comprehension*

1 (a) Why did Pa need a big spoon for use in his bullet making?

(b) Why was it important that the spoon should be 'long-handled' (line 3)?

2 (a) What was the purpose of 'the little hole in the bullet-mould' (line 9)?

(b) How did the hole affect the surface of the bullets and how did Pa deal with this?

3 What evidence can you find of Pa's keenness not to waste any lead?

4 Why did Pa clean his gun every evening?

5 What use did Pa make of the ramrod when cleaning the gun?

6 (a) Why did the water for cleaning the gun have to be boiling?

(b) How did Pa know when the barrel was clean?

7 What were the special uses, during cleaning operations, of (a) the clean cloth, (b) the clean greased rag, and (c) the clean, greased cloth?

8 What part did Laura and Mary play in the business of re-loading the gun?

9 (*a*) What part did the greased cloth play in re-loading the
    gun?
    (*b*) Why did this cloth have to be in little pieces?
10 Why did Pa need the ramrod again for re-loading the gun?
11 What was the trickiest part of the re-loading operation,
    and why?
12 (*a*) Where exactly was the loaded gun kept?
    (*b*) Why was it kept there?
    (*c*) What was the gun mainly used for, do you think?

B *Interpretation and criticism*

13 'He squatted on the hearth . . .' (line 5).
    How would you describe the action of 'squatting'?
14 'He trimmed off the little lumps . . .' (line 20).
    Why is the word 'trimmed' used here instead of, for in-
    stance, 'shaved'? (It is worth looking up the meanings of
    both words in a good dictionary.)
15 How does the formation of the word 'ramrod' (line 31) help
    to convey its meaning to someone reading or hearing the
    word for the first time?
16 What kind of movement is indicated by the use of the word
    'spurted' (line 37)?
17 (*a*) What will something 'sleek' (line 46) look and,
    perhaps, feel like?
    (*b*) When is the word 'sleek' used in connection with
    animals and with humans?
18 'He pounded them tightly against the powder' (line 67).
    What does the word 'pound' specially suggest that the word
    'hit' does not?
19 'Pa had whittled the hooks . . .' (line 80).
    What do you do when you 'whittle' wood?
20 How can you tell that the events in this passage took place
    many years ago – towards the end of the nineteenth cen-
    tury, in fact – and in a lonely isolated spot (in the United
    States)?
21 This passage is full of information about how Pa made his
    bullets, cleaned and loaded his gun. So much information
    could be boring – but the writer makes it full of interest.
    (*a*) How does she do this?
    (*b*) In what ways, particularly, does the presence of Laura
    and Mary add to the interest of the passage?

C *Ideas for writing*

22 Write a description, true or imaginary, funny or serious, about an occasion when you have helped Mum or Dad, a relative or friend, with a major job in the house – wallpapering, or painting, or repairing something, for instance.

23 'The gun was always loaded, and always above the door so that Pa could get it quickly and easily, any time he needed a gun.'
Bearing in mind that Pa lived in the 'little house in the big woods', write an imaginary story describing what happened on the next occasion Pa needed that gun!

D *Suggestions for reading*

This passage is taken from *Little House in the Big Woods*, the first of a series of books, all dealing with true happenings in the life of the American author Laura Ingalls Wilder. As a child Laura trekked westwards across the United States with her family in the pioneering days of the last quarter of the 19th century. The Little House was in the Big Woods of Wisconsin, where there were no roads, no people, only trees and wild animals – wolves, bears, wild cats, minks, otters.

From the woods of Wisconsin Laura and her family travelled westwards in a covered wagon into Indian country and these experiences are described in the second book, *Little House on the Prairie*. Their eventual settling in a little house built into a river bank and Laura's first experiences at school are described in the third book, *On the Banks of Plum Creek*. You can follow Laura's adventures as she grows up in the books which follow, *By the Shores of Silver Lake*, *The Long Winter* (Laura's tale of a hard fight for survival during a winter on the open prairie), *Little Town on the Prairie*, *These Happy Golden Years*, *Farmer Boy*, and *First Four Years*.

All these books by Laura Ingalls Wilder are available in Puffin paperbacks.

9
The birthday bike

Brock wanted a light-weight racing bike for his birthday but his father has bought him an old British Army bicycle.

Brock heard the key turn in the wash-house. Dad was taking his bike out. Brock leapt out of bed and went into his own room. Mum had laid out his clothes on the chair. In less than a minute he was dressed.

Then the gate banged. Brock jumped down the stairs two at a time.

'There's a surprise for you in the yard,' Mum said, as he burst into the kitchen. Brock's heart was thumping when he followed her through the back door.

10 'Close your eyes,' Mum told him with a laugh. She took his hand and led him into the sunlight.

'You can open them now.'

Brock hadn't known what to expect but he hadn't anticipated what he saw in front of him. The bike was propped against the wash-house wall. The frame tubing was thick and it was painted a dull, dark brown colour. Everywhere else was black. In places the paint had cracked, revealing patches of red rust underneath. The handlebars were perfectly straight and at each end was a black rubber grip. The saddle was the

20 broadest and the heaviest looking seat Brock had ever seen on a bike. It was adjusted to its lowest position. Tied to the brake-pipe was a card on which was printed:

Happy Birthday
with much love
from Mum and Dad

Brock knew Mum had done it by the small neat printing.

'Do you like it?' she asked him.

'I'm not sure,' Brock answered. He hesitated, not knowing what to say. Then he looked up and he saw the anxious expres-
30 sion on her face.

'It's really quite nice, I suppose,' he added.

'Have a ride and see what you think,' Mum told him. Brock nodded. He tried to smile, but really he felt hopeless. What would his friends say when they saw it? They'd make jokes and laugh at him about it.

Brock wheeled the bike through the gate onto the road. The frame was enormous and getting on was like mounting a horse. He wobbled along to the bottom of Churchill Street and then came back again. Fortunately the road was quiet so nobody
40 saw him. Brock was glad because every time the bike went over a bump it made a clanging sound. Mum was standing at the front window, smiling and nodding her head in approval.

'Breakfast in one minute,' she called.

Brock wheeled the bike over the curb. He tried to lift it over the low wall at the front of the house, but that was impossible. It was so incredibly heavy. He had to reach over the gate and release the catch. Even pushing the bike took all his effort.

'Here you are,' Mum said. 'Your breakfast is all ready.' Brock followed her into the house.
50 'There's a grapefruit on the table for you,' Mum told him. 'I've given you a whole one because it's your birthday.' Grapefruit was Brock's favourite fruit. Brock sat down at the table and stirred his hot chocolate. Mum came in with two slices of toast.

'I've arranged your birthday cards for you,' Mum said, indicating the row of cards on the mantelshelf. Brock hadn't noticed them before. The one of the penny-farthing[1] was the best.

'Have you any old cloths?' Brock asked. 'I want to clean my
60 bike.'

'I'm sure I can find you something,' Mum said brightly. She came back a few minutes later with some torn-up rags and a tin of polish.

'I thought you might like this as well.'

'Yes, all right,' Brock answered. He drank the last of the hot chocolate and stood up.

[1] an old-fashioned bicycle with a high and a low wheel.

'Now is there anything else, before I start work?' Mum asked.
'No, thank you.'
'Try to look a bit more cheerful,' Mum said. 'It is your birth-
70 day.' Brock nodded and walked past her into the back yard.
He spent the next two hours rubbing and polishing his bike.
At the end it hardly looked any different than it had at the
beginning. Brock threw the rag on the concrete and straighten-
ed his back. He had pins and needles in both legs and his
fingers were red and raw from rubbing. It hurt him even to
look at the bike. It was so cumbersome and ugly.
I wonder what Dad would say if I asked him to send it back,
Brock thought.
He sat on the dustbin and half closed his eyes, but the bike
80 was still just as terrible. It was while he was sitting there, that
David Whitman, the boy from next door, jumped over the
fence between the two houses. Whitman was fourteen and had
curly red hair. He stared in astonishment at Brock's bike.
'Hello, Titch,' he said, coming closer. Whitman called
Brock 'Titch' because he was so small. 'You don't mean to tell
me this is your new bike!' Brock didn't answer. He picked up a
piece of rag and polished the rim on the front wheel.
'You're wasting your time cleaning that,' Whitman said
scornfully.
90 Whitman built his own racing-bikes. Only last week he'd
finished building another one. Whitman collected all the parts
and then put them together himself. He was really brilliant at
it. He sold the last bike for thirty pounds. And he only had it a
few weeks before he found a buyer. The one he'd just built was
in his wash-house. It was white all over except for the alloy
parts. A boy named Brian Anderson called the day it was
finished. He offered twenty-two pounds, but Whitman said he
wasn't taking a penny less than thirty. Brock would have given
anything for a bike like that.
100 Brock added some more polish to the rag and started on the
handlebars.
'Come out of there,' Whitman told him, pushing Brock to
one side. He lifted the bike with one hand, held it still, groaned
and then pretended to collapse beneath the weight.
'Where did it come from?' he demanded, shaking the bike so
it made loud rattling sounds.
'My dad bought it from the army,' Brock explained. He

wished Whitman would go away and leave him alone.

'It looks like it,' Whitman said, laughing sarcastically. 'They
110 must have used it for a tank before they sent it to you.'

He turned the bike upside down and laid it on the concrete
path.

'The chain's too slack,' he observed grimly. 'And this frame's
buckled by the appearance of things.'

He wiped his hands disdainfully on a piece of rag. Then
without asking permission, he carried the bike into the street
and rode away on it.

Mum came rushing out of the front door, her hands covered
in flour. She was terribly upset.

120 'You shouldn't have let that boy ride your bike,' Mum said in
an agitated voice. 'What do you think Dad will say if he
damages it!'

'It won't happen again,' Brock promised. He felt completely
defeated. Mum looked anxiously down the road, wiped her
hands on her apron, and then went back into the house. Brock
sat on the edge of the curb and drew an outline of a racing-bike
in the dirt with the end of a sharp stone.

RICHARD POTTS
A Boy and his Bike

A Comprehension

1 What signs are there of Brock's excitement in the minutes
before he sees the bike?

2 What evidence is there in the passage of the bike's age and
its old-fashioned design?

3 What did Brock find unpleasant about the bike when he
took it out to try it?

4 Brock's Mum knew that Brock wanted a new racing bike
and knew that Brock would be disappointed with this bike.

(*a*) How can you tell that she is worried about how Brock
will react to the bike?

(*b*) In what ways does she try to make the morning of his
birthday as enjoyable as possible?

5 (*a*) How did Brock try to improve the appearance of the
bike?

(*b*) For what reasons did he try, do you think?
6 Why could Whitman in particular be expected to be critical of Brock's bike?
7 What were Whitman's main criticisms of the bike?
8 What evidence is there to suggest that Whitman fancies himself as a bit of an expert on bikes?
9 (*a*) Why did Brock feel 'completely defeated' (line 123)?
(*b*) Why did he draw 'an outline of a racing bike in the dirt' (line 126), do you think?

B *Interpretation and criticism*

10 'Leapt' (line 2), 'jumped' (line 5), 'burst' (line 8).
What impressions of Brock does the writer intend to convey by using these words to describe Brock's actions?
11 Brock's ambition had been to have a light-weight modern racing bike. Discuss the description of the bike (lines 14 to 21). How does the writer use descriptive detail to emphasise to us that the bike was everything that Brock did *not* want in a bike?
12 What is the point of the observation that the bike seat 'was adjusted to its lowest position' (line 21), do you think?
13 It is often interesting to consider *why* people make particular remarks and to wonder what they are thinking as they make them.
(*a*) What lies behind Brock's Mum's question 'Do you like it?' (line 27).
(*b*) What lies behind her suggestion 'Have a ride and see what you think' (line 32)?
(*c*) What thoughts may be running through Brock's mind when he says 'It's really quite nice, I suppose' (line 31)?
14 What impressions are conveyed to the reader by the remark that 'getting on was like mounting a horse' (line 37)?
15 What might Mum be thinking and, perhaps, hoping when she stood at the front window 'smiling and nodding her head in approval' (line 42)?
16 Discuss what Mum's behaviour and remarks to Brock at breakfast time may indicate about her thoughts and feelings then.
17 Why does she speak 'brightly' (line 61) when she observes

'I'm sure I can find you something'?
18 Look up the meaning of the word 'cumbersome' (line 76) in a good dictionary.
From the details given in the passage in what ways was the bike 'cumbersome'?
19 (a) Why does Whitman speak 'scornfully' (line 89) and laugh 'sarcastically' (line 109) as he inspects the bike?
(b) What is revealed of Whitman's attitude towards the bike in the statement 'He wiped his hands *disdainfully*' (line 115)?
20 Discuss the reasons why Brock 'felt completely defeated' (line 123) after facing Whitman's scorn and after Whitman has ridden off to try his bike.

C Ideas for writing

21 Brock was disappointed with his first bike; you may have been luckier. Think of some the most outstanding 'firsts' in your life – perhaps your first bike, or first flight in an aeroplane, or first holiday abroad, first riding lesson, first really adult clothes, first present of a proper football or cricket bat or tennis racquet. Write about the occasion – the events leading up to it, your feelings on achieving this 'first', and the adventures or experiences connected with it afterwards.
22 All of us have at some time been terribly disappointed by a present or by an experience which we have been looking forward to for a long time. Describe one such disappointment in your own life – starting with the hopes you had beforehand, then describing in detail the time of disappointment, and finally telling what happened afterwards as a result.

D Suggestions for reading

This passage is taken from the novel *A Boy and his Bike* by Richard Potts. It is a sensitive and understanding tale of Brock's hopes and disappointments concerning his first bike. However, if you read the book you will find that Brock tries to make the most of his ex-army bike, and eventually manages to get his racing bike. There are troubles to be faced and conquered even then, however. *A Boy and his Bike* has been published as a Puffin paperback.

If your ambition has been not for a bike but for a dog, try Philippa Pearce's short novel about a young boy's intense longing for a dog, entitled *A Dog So Small*. This is available as a Puffin paperback.

Hopes and ambitions of a very different kind feature in the popular story of a girl's hopes to become a ballet dancer, *Ballet Shoes*, by Noel Streatfeild, also available in Puffin paperback.

10
The buckjumping show

Naturally, with horses playing such a big part in everyone's life, any entertainment like a buckjumping show had to be very good indeed. One of these shows was more famous than any of the others, for the star horse was considered the savagest buck-jumper in the country, and the man who rode him an unbeatable rider. So when it got around that this man, Billy Weight, and his horse Bobs were coming to the Show we looked forward to it very much indeed. There were to be other sideshows and the inevitable merry-go-round. Strange to think
10 that bush children who rode so many real horses were so ex-cited about climbing on to little wooden horses, and being whirled round and round to the hurdy-gurdy music of the calliope![1] Of course you have to remember that most bush children had not seen a train, or even a tall building, or the sea, and these little shows held all the glamour and excitement of the year for them.

When this particular show opened my father and I drove to it in a car that was rather like one of today's shooting brakes, but we just called it the truck. The sides were netted in, so that
20 the dogs could ride in there, and we took them nearly any-where with us. They hated staying at home, and in the truck they would simply lie down and sleep when we left them.

When we reached the show my father and I started around the sideshows, leaving the dogs in the truck. We laughed at ourselves and each other in the distorting mirrors, and I had a ride on the merry-go-round. We called on an old friend, the snake-handler, who was wading about the snake pit in a pair of pink knitted bootees, through which, he claimed, the snakes could not get their fangs.

[1] steam-organ

46

30   Then it was time for the buckjumping show, and it seemed
that the tent held every bushman for miles around, because in
a country of fine riders Billy Weight was considered the finest
of them all. He was a half-caste (these men are often wonderful
riders) and Bobs, his horse, was unique. Real buckjumpers are
very rare. Lots of horses buck in a way, but it is mostly what is
called pigrooting, they put their heads down, arch their backs
and jump along in a stiff-legged way. This is fairly hard to sit,
but the *real* buckjumper is almost unrideable, for it gives a sort
of twist to its body in mid-air, all four feet off the ground. Bobs
40   was the real thing, and some of the finest riders in Australia
could not sit him.
      Inside the buckjumping tent, the ring was quite a small one
of trodden-down earth, surrounded by a strong rail fence to
keep the bucking horses from breaking through – this
sometimes happened anyhow! The tent was lit by smoke flares.
There were no seats, everybody stood, and the tent was packed
with tough, leathery bushmen waiting to see this rider who was
supposed to be better than themselves. Most of the crowd knew
my father, and they let me wriggle through their legs until I
50   was beside the ring; then one man lifted me up and perched
me on his shoulder.
      In films of American rodeos, the horses are saddled and
mounted in a horse-sized yard we called a 'crush', so that they
cannot plunge about; but that is not the way we do it in
Australia. There the saddle may be put on in the crush, and it
is a slippery 'poly' saddle without knee-pads, something like a
large racing saddle; then the gate of the crush is opened, the
horse dashes out, and is mounted free in the ring.
      From where I was perched on a tall bushman's shoulder I
60   saw Bobs come charging into the ring. He was a great bay,
eighteen hands high, glistening with sweat and fury. Then Billy Weight slipped into the ring. He was a small man, lithe as a
cat, an old felt hat in one hand, and soft-soled sneakers on his
feet. Bobs reared and plunged, and when he was ready Billy
ran a few steps across the ring and sprang high on that
twisting, rolling demon's body. He shouted and hit the horse
with his old hat, and the intensity and savagery of the horse's
tremendous twisting leaps were thrilling to watch. The
bushmen around me *knew* how great a rider this man was.
70   When Billy thought Bobs had had enough he slipped to the

47

ground, the gates opened, and Bobs charged out again. It was as though a bolt of lightning had left the ring; once again it was just a dimly-lit, earth-floored circle.

MARY ELWYN PATCHETT
Ajax the Warrior

A Comprehension

1 Why was the writer so keen to go to the buckjumping show described in this passage?
2 What attractions other than the buckjumping did the bush children enjoy at these shows?
3 Why did the bush children enjoy these attractions?
4 What proof is there in the passage that the writer and her companions lived in a very remote inland part of Australia?
5 Why was a motor truck more useful than a car for the writer's family?
6 Explain in your own words the special qualities possessed by the horse Bobs which drew so many bushmen to the show to see him perform.
7 Why were the bushmen also particularly keen to see the rider Billy Weight?
8 How did the writer manage to get a good view of the buck-jumping?
9 What is the most important difference, according to the writer, between the preparation of the horse for the ride in American rodeos and the preparation at the Australian buckjumping show?
10 Try to explain clearly and simply why the horse in these shows is called a 'buckjumper'.

B Interpretation and criticism

11 (*a*) What is a 'merry-go-round' (line 9) and what is a 'hurdy-gurdy' (line 12)?
  (*b*) Why do both these words suit the objects they name?
12 What kind of movement and speed of movement do you associate with the word 'whirled' (line 12)?
13 (*a*) What are 'sideshows' (line 9)?

(*b*) Why are they so called, do you think?

14 (*a*) Look up the precise meaning of the word 'glamour' (line 15) in a good dictionary.

(*b*) In what ways did the little side-shows have 'glamour' for the bush children?

15 Describe some of the effects created by 'distorting mirrors' (line 25).

16 Sometimes people will invent a word in order to make an explanation of something clearer. What, then, must horses at buckjumping shows *look* like and *move* like when they are 'pigrooting' (line 36)?

17 What would the bushmen *look* like if they can be described as 'leathery' (line 47)?

18 What sort of position is someone in when they are 'perched' (line 59)?

19 Describe the sort of movements Billy Weight might have made if he could be described as being 'lithe as a cat' (line 62).

20 (*a*) What kind of shoes would you *expect* 'sneakers' (line 63) to be?

(*b*) Why did Billy probably wear '*soft-soled*' sneakers?

21 How does the writer bring Bobs and Billy to life in your imagination as you read the passage?

C Ideas for writing

22 Billy Weight entertained his spectators at the buckjumping show by his agility and skill in riding an almost unrideable horse. Write an account of any occasions when you have enjoyed watching someone who entertains by performing difficult feats involving agility and skill – riding a horse or motor cycle, driving a car, walking a tight-rope, balancing in precarious positions, for instance. Describe the skills, the actions and the tricky movements involved, and describe also your reactions and those of other spectators to the display.

23 Imagine yourself to be the daring entertainer – or, rather, an entertainer who has given up because you have lost your skill and agility, or your nerve – looking back on your career. Describe some of your most successful enter-tainments (or 'stunts') when you were at the height of your

powers and conclude your account with a description of the disastrous performance which made you realise that it was time to give up!

D Suggestions for reading

Mary Elwyn Patchett's *Ajax The Warrior*, from which this passage comes, is a true account of the writer's childhood on an Australian cattle station. 'Ajax is one of her three dogs, a devoted friend who twice saved her life. This is a most exciting book about life in the Australian bush.

If you like *Ajax The Warrior*, then try also Mary Elwyn Patchett's two novels, also set in the Australian outback, *The Brumby* and *Come Home, Brumby*. All three books have been published in Puffin paperbacks. The hardbacks were first published by Lutterworth Press.

An unusual and thought-provoking story of the adventures of two children, sole survivors of a plane crash, in the Australian bush, is James Vance Marshall's *Walkabout*, available as a Peacock paperback. (This book has appeared elsewhere under the title *The Children*.)

11
The Thing

The Thing itself lay almost entirely buried in sand, amidst the scattered splinters of a fir tree it had shivered to fragments in its descent. The uncovered part had the appearance of a huge cylinder, caked over, and its outline softened by a thick, scaly, dun-coloured incrustation. It had a diameter of about thirty yards. He approached the mass, surprised at the size and more so at the shape, since most meteorites are rounded more or less completely. It was, however, still so hot from its flight through the air as to forbid his near approach. A stirring noise within
10 its cylinder he ascribed to the unequal cooling of its surface; for at that time it had not occurred to him that it might be hollow.

He remained standing at the edge of the pit that the thing had made for itself, staring at its strange appearance, astonished chiefly at its unusual shape and colour, and dimly perceiving even then some evidence of design in its arrival. The early morning was wonderfully still, and the sun, just clearing the pine trees towards Weybridge, was already warm. He did not remember hearing any birds that morning, there was certainly no breeze stirring, and the only sounds were the faint
20 movements from within the cindery cylinder. He was all alone on the common.

Then suddenly he noticed with a start that some of the grey clinker, the ashy incrustation that covered the meteorite, was falling off the circular edge of the end. It was dropping off in flakes and raining down upon the sand. A large piece suddenly came off and fell with a sharp noise that brought his heart into his mouth.

For a minute he scarcely realised what this meant, and, although the heat was excessive, he clambered down into the
30 pit close to the bulk to see the thing more clearly. He fancied even then that the cooling of the body might account for this,

but what disturbed that idea was the fact that the ash was falling only from the end of the cylinder.
   And then he perceived that, very slowly, the circular top of
the cylinder was rotating on its body. It was such a gradual
movement that he discovered it only through noticing that a
black mark that had been near him five minutes ago was now
at the other side of the circumference. Even then he scarcely
understood what this indicated, until he heard a muffled
40 grating sound and saw the black mark jerk forward an inch or
so. Then the thing came upon him in a flash. The cylinder was
artificial – hollow – with an end that screwed out! Something
within the cylinder was unscrewing the top!

H.G. WELLS
The War of the Worlds

A *Comprehension*

1 Describe in your own words the location of The Thing
   when discovered by the man, and the surroundings in
   which it had fallen.
2 How did the conditions at the scene make it easier for the
   man to listen to the noises coming from the cylinder?
3 What did the man think The Thing was at first and what
   made him change his mind?
4 Why did he not move close to The Thing at first?
5 What eventually made him decide to move closer to The
   Thing?
6 How at first did he account for the flakes of clinker falling
   off the cylinder?
7 What observation quickly proved his theory about the
   flakes to be wrong?
8 When did it first become clear to the man that the top of
   the cylinder was rotating?
9 Why was the cylinder rotating and what happened to make
   the man realise why it was doing so?
10 'The cylinder was artificial' (line 42).
   What terrible implications would be clear to the man once
   he had realised this?
11 What, then, was The Thing?

B *Interpretation and criticism*

12 How does the writer's description of the fir tree in the first sentence of the passage emphasise the speed and force of The Thing's impact?

13 Why does the reference to the cylinder as 'The Thing' at the beginning of the passage immediately introduce a sinister note?

14 (*a*) Which phrase in the second paragraph of this passage suggests that the man suspected that the arrival of The Thing at this time and at this spot may have been planned?
(*b*) Why did the time, and the spot where it landed, make him suspect this?

15 Why does the writer describe the cylinder as 'cindery' in line 20?

16 Why does the brief statement 'He was all alone on the common' (line 20) help to make the passage more exciting?

17 'He clambered down into the pit close to the bulk . . .' (line 29).
(*a*) What does the word 'clambered' suggest about the size of the pit and about his movements down *into* the pit?
(*b*) What does the word 'bulk' suggest about the cylinder when seen from within the pit?

18 'He heard a muffled grating sound' (line 39).
(*a*) What are the special qualities of a 'muffled' sound?
(*b*) Why was the 'grating sound' at first 'muffled', here?

19 Exclamation marks are better if used sparingly, as they are in this passage. What effect is the writer creating by reserving their use until the last two sentences of this passage? Why are the marks obviously necessary to end both sentences?

20 The book from which this passage is taken was first published in 1898. Why does it still make interesting reading today? How does the writer create the tension at the beginning and then maintain it right up to the end?

C *Ideas for writing*

21 'Something within the cylinder was unscrewing the top!' Try writing a continuation of this story, an exciting episode which leads to another frightening climax where *you* leave *your* readers itching to know what happens next!

53

22 The passage you have been studying was written at the end of the last century. Write a piece of similar length in which, in the light of our present knowledge of space travel, you describe the arrival of a new 'Thing' and the start of an invasion from outer space. Choose, perhaps, a lonely spot in your home area as the site of the first landing.

D Suggestions for reading

Science fiction novels written by H.G. Wells at the end of the nineteenth century and the beginning of the twentieth century still make fascinating reading, even though the real thing has turned out differently from the fiction. *The War of the Worlds*, from which this passage is taken, is still worth reading through; if you decide to sample a chapter first, try the one entitled 'Dead London'. It is available as a Pan paperback.

Amongst Wells's science fiction, *The Time Machine* is available as an Everyman paperback, whilst *War in the Air* is available as a Penguin paperback. You may be both amused and entertained by H. G. Wells's method of getting to the moon in *The First Men in the Moon*, available in Fontana Paperback. Also available in Fontana is the equally entertaining tale *The Invisible Man*.

Science fiction today is very different. There are some contemporary science fiction stories listed in the Suggestions for reading on page 10.

12
Jet starts his training

The first job Mr Reynolds was set to do was to build the play-house to replace the one Lotty had given up in the coal-shed. She was happy with the exchange, and the dogs were housed in conditions more suited to dogs in training; for keeping them in the house made them soft and spoiled them for hard work.

Next, on his wife's instructions, and after a visit to the dog-track, Mr Reynolds designed and made a trap that was set up in the yard, but that was collapsible and light enough to carry out to the park when the dogs went there for exercise.

10 'Why do they need that, mammy?' Lotty asked.

'They got to learn to accept bein' put in there before the race start, and they has to learn to come shootin' out when the hare goes past an' the door is opened for them.'

But the trap was no good without a hare. It was all right in the yard where Peter could work the lure, dragging it quickly past the trap for David to release the dog from inside to spring and run and pounce. But the problem was to keep him run-ning, and this was where Mr Reynolds's best piece of gadgetry came in. Again, he had to work from advice, but once he had

20 been told the principle of the machinery they needed, the rest was easy. Peter went round the scrap-yards and bought an old bicycle frame with pedals and chain still good. Mr Reynolds at-tached a drum-like cylinder to the rear cog, and made the frame to stand stable when turned upside-down, with steel struts for legs in place of the seat and the handlebars. Now, when the pedals were turned like a handle, the drum turned. A length of strong string with the stuffed rabbit at the end of it was fastened to the drum, so that when the pedals turned at speed the string would wind round the drum and, as it reeled

30 in, it pulled the lure along fast enough to give the dogs a run.

A last piece of necessary equipment was a muzzle for the puppy. When dogs went on the track they had to wear muzzles because any bickering and snapping among them could obviously spoil the race. Mr Reynolds bought a muzzle, and with patient effort they persuaded Jet to accept it as regular wear when he ran.

David went along with Peter and his dad to help at the first trial they held in the park. It needed one person to work the machine, and it was easier when two started the dogs. Peter
40 worked the machine, David put Allegro into the trap, and his dad held Jet alongside. As the hare flashed by, David sprang the trap, and Mr Reynolds let Jet slip, all in a moment.

Allegro knew what to do; she shot from the trap and went hurtling, low to the ground, with kicking heels. Her body seemed to fold and stretch with a tremendous thrust from her back legs; and, with each rapid, wavy repetition of the movement, she kicked up tufts of grass and soft earth behind her all the way. In direct line she sped after the bobbing hare, until, at the end of its course, she over-ran it as the machine slowed.
50 Then she turned, arcing back towards Peter, to be patted for her efforts.

Jet did not show any of his mother's urgency that first time; he was unfamiliar with this routine and went bounding off gamely, yet playfully, in pursuit of Allegro. It was only when he realised that this was serious running that he laid his ears back and tracked her from behind. He was too young and too small yet to match her speed, but it gave David a queer, excited feeling to see this young, black dog running all-out for the first time. How strange it was that he had such an instinct
60 for running, and was gifted with the perfect action, untaught and unpractised.

'Gifted' – David thought again of the word he had used, and felt an odd sense that Jet was unusual. He knew nothing about racing-dogs; but there was such fluency in this puppy's movement, and such an air of assurance about him – he looked perfect, unflawed from the black tip of his nose to the black tip of his tail – that David knew he must be special.

GEOFFREY KILNER
Jet, a Gift to the Family

A Comprehension

1 What evidence is there in the passage that all the Reynolds family are interested in preparing for the training of the greyhounds?

2 Where were the greyhounds to be kept, and why was this?

3 What indications are there in the passage that Mr Reynolds was prepared to take advice over the designing of his gadgets?

4 What evidence is there of Mr Reynolds's practical skill in making things once the design has been worked out?

5 (*a*) What training could take place in the yard at the back of the house?
  (*b*) Why did training in the yard have severe limitations?

6 What were the special uses of (a) the drum and (b) the bicycle pedals in the gadget used to operate the 'lure'?

7 What did the family use as the 'lure'?

8 What evidence is there that good team work was necessary in the practice sessions with the trap and with the machine?

9 (*a*) How does Allegro reveal her experience in the first trial at the park?
  (*b*) How does Jet reveal his *in*experience?

10 In what ways does Jet reveal to David his great promise as a racing greyhound, at this first trial?

11 What impressions of the Reynolds family do you gain from reading this passage?

B Interpretation and criticism

12 For what reasons was 'Jet' a good name to give the dog?

13 Use a good dictionary to discover the origins of the word 'lure' (line 15).
  (*a*) How do the uses of the 'lure' in greyhound training and racing differ from the use of the 'lure' in falconry?
  (*b*) With the help of the dictionary discuss some of the uses of the word 'lure' and the word 'alluring' when connected with *human* behaviour. How do these uses link up with the original meaning of the word?

14 Try to explain the actions involved in a 'pounce' (line 17).

15 'This was where Mr Reynolds's best piece of gadgetry came in' (line 18).

(a) What is a 'gadget' and what qualities might you expect to find in someone who designs and builds gadgets?

(b) Why was it necessary for 'the frame to stand *stable* when turned upside-down' in the case of Mr Reynolds's gadget?

16 (a) What is a 'strut'?

(b) Why did Mr Reynolds's gadget need '*steel struts* for legs' (line 24)?

(c) Can you explain why the word 'strut' is used to describe a particular manner of walking?

17 Look at the paragraph describing Allegro's behaviour when released from the trap (lines 43 to 51). How does the writer's choice of words to describe her *movements* illustrate effectively that 'Allegro knew what to do' (line 43)?

18 'Jet . . . went bounding off gamely, yet playfully, in pursuit of Allegro' (line 53).

In what ways does this statement help to suggest that at the start of his training Jet didn't realise 'that this was serious running'?

19 (a) What are we suggesting if we claim that an animal – or person – is 'gifted' (line 60)?

(b) Why does it seem that Jet may be 'gifted', judging from the evidence here?

20 Look up the meanings of the word 'fluent' in a good dictionary. What does the writer mean when he observes that there was 'such *fluency* in this puppy's movement' (line 64)?

21 How does the writer help his readers to become as interested in the gadgets and the training as the Reynolds family is in the story?

C Ideas for writing

22 This passage reveals something of the pleasure gained from a whole family's being interested in a particular activity. Write about an occasion, real or imaginary, when you enjoyed being a member of a group (family, relatives, or friends) involved in an enjoyable activity – an 'activity' holiday, training for a competition, producing a play, organising a team, for instance.

23 Have you ever solved a problem by designing and making a gadget? Write about an occasion, real or imaginary, when

you did so. If you are a brilliant inventor it will be a success story: your gadget works perfectly. If you aren't an inventive person – and many of us are not – your story will, of course, be different: you try out your gadget and manage to be amused by the hilarious results!

D *Suggestions for reading*

This passage comes from Geoffrey Kilner's unusual and fascinating novel *Jet, a Gift to the Family*. On impulse, Mr Reynolds has bought a greyhound 'dog' – but the 'dog' turns out to be pregnant. The family hope for a number of puppies which they can sell to recoup the cost of Allegro. They are all disappointed when only one puppy – a black one – is born. However, Jet, the black puppy, may have a 'gift' for racing. A fortune teller has told Mr Reynolds mysteriously that 'Black is a gift'. Does this mean that Jet will be a great race winner? The story charts Jet's progress and the adventures that befall the Reynolds family, especially young David, when they become involved in the intrigues of the greyhound racing world.

The book is available as a Puffin paperback.

If you like making things yourself then there are some interesting books in the series called 'Practical Puffins' – all paperbacks. They include *Carpentry, Constructions: Big Things to Make, Cooking, Cover-Ups: Things to Put on Yourself, Presents: Making Them to Match People, Gardening,* and *Kites*.

13
Marianne dreamed

Marianne dreamed.

    She was in a great open stretch of country, flat like a prairie, covered, as far as she could see, with the long dry grass in which she was standing more than knee deep. There were no roads, no paths, no hills and no valleys. Only the prairie stretched before her on all sides till it met the grey encircling sky. Here and there it was dotted with great stones or rocks, which rose just above the level of the tall grass, like heads peering from all directions

10   Marianne stood and looked. There seemed to be nothing to do and nowhere to go. Wherever she looked she saw nothing but grass and stones and sky, the same on every side of her. Yet something, a nagging uneasiness which she could not account for, drove her to start walking; and because at one point on the skyline she thought she could see something like a faint trickle of smoke, she walked towards that.

    The ground under her feet was rutted and uneven, and the grass harsh and prickling. She could not move fast, and it seemed that she had walked a long way before she saw that she

20 had been right about the faint line in the sky. It was a wavering stream of smoke, rising in the windless air from the chimney of a house.

    It was a curious looking house, with leaning walls, its windows and door blank and shut. It rose unexpectedly straight from the prairie; a low uneven fence separated its small plot from the surrounding ground, though the coarse grass was the same within and without. There were some large pale yellow flowers about, which Marianne could not recognise, growing a foot or two high; they seemed to be as much outside the fence

30 as in, and certainly did not constitute a garden. Nothing mov-

ed except the thread of smoke rising from the chimney. In all
that vast expanse nothing else moved.

There was a gate in the fence. Marianne pushed it open and
walked up the path to the door. She did not much like the look
of the house, with its blank staring windows and its bare front
door, but she liked the prairie even less.

'I must get in,' said Marianne aloud in her dream. 'I've got
to get in.'

There was no knocker and there was no bell. Marianne
40 knocked with her knuckles, but it was a disappointing little
noise and she was not surprised that no one answered. She
looked around for a stone to beat on the door but the only
stones were the great grey boulders outside the fence. As she
stood, considering what to do, she heard the distant sound of
wind. Across the prairie it blew towards her, and in its path the
grass whistled and rustled, dry stalk on dry stalk, and bent, so
that she could see the path of the wind as it approached her.
Then it was all around her, and everything that had been so
still before became alive with movement. The grass writhed
50 and tore at its roots, the pale flowers beat against their stems,
the thin thread of smoke was blown out like a candle flame,
and disappeared into the dark sky. The wind whistled round
the house and was gone, leaving Marianne deaf for a moment,
and suddenly chilled.

'I'm frightened here,' she said. 'I've got to get away from the
grass and the stones and the wind. I've got to get into the
house.'

No voice spoke in reply to her words, and there was no signal
from the silent house; but she knew the answer as if she had
60 heard it.

'I could get in,' Marianne thought, 'if there was a person inside the house. There has got to be a person. I can't get in
unless there is somebody there.'

'Why isn't there someone in the house?' she cried to the empty world around her.

'Put someone there,' the silent answer said.

'How can I?' Marianne protested. 'How can I put someone in
the house? I can't get in myself! And I've got to get in!'

'I've got to get in!' she heard herself say, and the words woke
70 her up. With difficulty she struggled back to realise that the
house and prairie were gone: she was lying in bed, and the

memory of the six weeks more to be spent there was lying in wait for her, to weigh down her spirits as soon as she was sufficiently awake to remember.

CATHERINE STORR
Marianne Dreams

A Comprehension

1 Why did the countryside of Marianne's dream appear to resemble a prairie?

2 What was distinctly unusual about the surface appearance of the grassland?

3 What was it about the prairie which probably prompted Marianne's feeling that 'there seemed to be nothing to do and nowhere to go' (line 10)?

4 Can *you* account for Marianne's 'nagging uneasiness' (line 13) about the surroundings in which she found herself?

5 Why did Marianne set off walking?

6 What did she find strange about the plot of ground inside the cottage fence?

7 Why did Marianne 'not much like the look of the house' (line 34)?

8 (*a*) Why, perhaps, did she have the urge to get inside the house?
(*b*) Why did she look round for a stone to beat on the door?

9 How did the sudden appearance and disappearance of the wind make Marianne's experience more frightening?

10 What probably helped to break Marianne's dream?

B Interpretation and criticism

11 'There were *no* roads, *no* paths, *no* hills and *no* valleys' (line 4).
What do all the negatives in this sentence convey to your imagination when you are reading it?

12 What effects are created by the description of the sky as 'grey' and 'encircling' (line 6)? In what ways would the atmosphere have seemed different had the sky been 'blue'?

13 'Here and there it was dotted with great stones or rocks' (line 7).
How does this statement help to emphasise how vast the prairie seemed to Marianne as she stood there?

14 'Like heads peering from all directions' (line 8).
(a) What qualities does this comparison give to the stones?
(b) What is the effect of this comparison in this lonely situation?
(c) What special effect is created by the use of the word 'peering'?

15 (a) Why is the smoke described as a 'faint trickle' on line 15, but as 'a wavering stream' on line 20?
(b) What similarity and what difference is there between the two words 'trickle' and 'stream'?

16 (a) What effect is created in your imagination by the observations '*Nothing moved* except the thread of smoke rising from the chimney. In all that vast expanse *nothing else moved*' (line 31)?
(b) Discuss the circumstances in which *stillness* can raise tension, both in stories and in real life.

17 Why do the 'blank staring windows' (line 35) and the 'bare front door' (line 35) create a rather disturbing and even frightening effect?

18 (a) How does the writer create the impression that the sudden wind was directed at Marianne and had something to do with her presence outside the house?
(b) How does the writer help her readers to share Marianne's feelings of fright as the wind whips up around her?
(c) What special impression is conveyed by the use of the word 'writhed' in the statement 'The grass *writhed* and tore at its roots . . .' (line 49)?

19 'I've got to get away from the grass and the stones and the wind' (line 55).
Sum up the ways in which the writer focusses your imagination on grass, stones and wind in the passage so that you can understand just why Marianne felt so frightened.

20 Discuss the features of Marianne's dream which strike you as being typical of the ways in which places and objects can appear in dreams and typical of the ways in which you become frightened in dreams of this kind.

C *Ideas for writing*

21 Think of a landscape which you know well – either in the
country or a park or open space in a town. Imagine
yourself to be having a dream in which you find yourself in
this landscape. In your dream world it seems strangely and
frighteningly different. Write a story about this dream in
which you describe this scene, its effects on you, and the
events connected with it which lead to a terrifying climax
just before, like Marianne, you wake up.

22 Dreams and nightmares are often hard to remember in
detail – so make one up instead. Imagine that you have
been watching a disturbing and frightening film or reading
a frightening story late at night. You go to bed and dream.
You find *yourself* in the film or story, playing a prominent
part. Write the story of *your* nightmare (which will
naturally be significantly different in many ways from the
film or story), showing how the original story got mixed up
in your dream.

D *Suggestions for reading*

This passage is taken from Catherine Storr's novel *Marianne
Dreams*. Marianne, confined to bed for many weeks, takes up
drawing, using a strange pencil found in an old workbox. She
finds that she can dream about what she draws. The passage
describes Marianne's first dream. In that dream you will
remember that when Marianne asked why there was no one in
the house the silent answer said 'Put someone there.' Marianne
added a drawing of a boy in an upstairs room of the cottage
and met the boy, Mark, in her next dream. However, by her
drawing, she has confined Mark, who is also ill, to the cottage.
Only Marianne can make him recover (or make him die) and
she can only do so through her drawings. Meanwhile, in real
life, a boy called Mark is also ill, and it seems as if Marianne's
drawings hold *his* fate in the balance too . . . .

Marianne Dreams is available as a Puffin paperback.

If you enjoy reading stories which are not only about
imaginative children but which will give your own imagination
plenty to think about, try the stories by Lucy M. Boston, starting, perhaps, with *The Children of Green Knowe* and *The
Chimneys of Green Knowe*, both published in Puffin paperbacks.

14
Across the Channel
by flying machine

The new machine was not ready until four o'clock in the afternoon, by which time the sky had clouded over slightly, and
Christina's stomach had contracted again. Will took the
machine up for a trial flight while she wound up her hair again
and buttoned herself back into her flying clothes. There was no
argument against not going, for the visibility was good, and the
wind light. The French mechanics were very kind, making
gallant remarks (she thought), to which she had to smile back,
although her smile already had the frozen feel about it that she
10 could remember sensing before. She had to stand there,
waiting, being calm, loathing every slow minute. But all was
well. Will was very happy with the new machine; they said
good-bye and shook hands all round, and then they were away
once more, heading for Calais.

This time the crossing was uneventful, although the weather
rapidly deteriorated as they reached the English coast. The
cloud came lower, no longer fleecy, but grey and miserable-
looking, pushed by an increasing wind. It was April weather,
the sun skimming over green downs and disappearing into
20 darkness, a white house almost flashing here and there, and
the shadows running like galloping horses. Christina could feel
the aircraft buffeted by the wind like a ship by green seas. It
lurched and rolled, and she held on to the sides of the cockpit
in horror, never having realised before that such things went
on up aloft. Will had no hands to pass notes with, fully oc-
cupied with keeping the machine on a level keel, but Christina
had to do her best with her maps, peering and checking and
trying to ignore the awful nausea in her stomach. At Ashford
there were two railway lines and two rivers, and innumerable
30 shining streams to confuse. The machine dropped twenty feet
like a stone and she almost lost the map, and certainly her dinner, moaning over the side of the cockpit. The compass needle

65

was going round in circles. A town appeared below, and she was forced to write, 'Tonbridge or Maidstone?' but as she passed the note over Will's shoulder the cloud blotted out the whole landscape and Will put the nose down and started to glide down. The rain stung Christina's face, hammering on the fuselage and wings with a noise like a drum to accompany the screaming of the wires. Will shouted over his shoulder, 'We'll
40 have to find somewhere to land when the squall's over. It'll be dark soon. Look out for a good place!' He had pushed his goggles up in order to see, and the rain was pouring over him as if they were under a waterfall. Christina could feel it going through her scarves and trickling down her neck. She peered over the side of the cockpit, moaning softly with all this new misery, and saw the ground blurry and swirling below, all woods and hedges and lumps and clutter. Will flattened out and they flew on beneath the fringes of the cloud, the rain like ice needles darting into the skin. For a moment the setting sun
50 shone wildly in their faces, all amongst the rain, so that the wings suddenly looked like flames dancing with water. Then a black cloud shut it out, and Christina realised that the day was finished. The ground was grey and disappearing, a light shining here and there, and they were marooned in the sky like outcasts.

William started to lose height, making big serpentine turns, looking for suitable ground. The squall had passed, the wind had dropped, and the evening was all damp and still in its fickle April manner, sorry for its outburst. Christina's teeth
60 were chattering with cold. She looked down, but Will had dropped into one of his tight corkscrew descents, and she could not bear it. All her insides corkscrewed in sympathy, and she shut her lips tight, ground her teeth, and hid her face in her hands. Will did not need her help in looking. He could do his own looking. She braced herself, remembering Sandy's words: 'The idea is that you pull out before you hit the ground.'

Amazingly, she felt nothing. A final swoop lifted her stomach, but gently, and then the soft bounce of the impact and a smooth, short run to a standstill. The undercarriage
70 sighed, and there was silence, save for the sound of dripping water. She opened her eyes.

'It's not Hendon,' Will was saying. 'But I'm not complaining.'

There were no welcoming crowds waiting to offer help in the damp, empty landscape that stretched out all round them. The only building in sight was a dilapidated barn. There was no friendly farm, no light to be seen, not even a road or a lane. Just sodden pasture, and over a hedge some cows regarding them without interest. Christina stepped down, and felt her
80 shoes fill with mud.
'Ugh!'

K.M. PEYTON
The Edge of the Cloud

A *Comprehension*

1 What evidence is there in the first paragraph that Christina is rather uneasy about the flight back across the English Channel?

2 Why did Christina and Will not set off back to England as soon as the plane was ready at four o' clock?

3 (*a*) Why were weather conditions favourable for the flight before they started?
(*b*) In what ways did weather conditions change during the flight?

4 How did the changing weather conditions affect the plane during the flight?

5 What evidence is there in the passage that there was no protection from the weather when flying in this early aeroplane?

6 What tasks did Christina have to perform during the flight?

7 In what ways did the weather, the time of day, and the difficulty of recognising features on the ground all make Christina's tasks more difficult?

8 What made Christina uncomfortable once William had decided to look for somewhere to land?

9 What proof is there that the plane made a good landing?

10 What kind of surface did the plane land on and in what sort of surroundings?

11 Sum up the main evidence in this passage which proves that this flight was made in the very early days of flying.

B *Interpretation and criticism*

12 Look up the meanings of the word 'gallant' in a good dictionary.

(*a*) What does the word 'gallant' mean when it is used, as here (line 8), in connection with 'gallant remarks' made by a man (or men) to a woman?

(*b*) What sort of 'gallant remarks' might the French mechanics have made to Christina in the circumstances?

(*c*) What indication is there in the passage that Christina may not have understood the words of the Frenchmen?

13 The aircraft was 'buffeted by the wind like a ship by green seas' (line 22).

(*a*) What happens when something is 'buffeted'?

(*b*) What does the comparison 'like a ship by green seas' help to tell you about the force of the wind's buffeting?

14 What sort of movements were involved when the plane 'lurched' (line 23)?

15 What problems was Christina having with her maps if she was 'peering' at them (line 27)?

16 How does the writer emphasise the heaviness, the noise and the general unpleasantness of the rain in her description of the squall they flew through? (Note, particularly, two vivid comparisons used in her description.)

Look up the meaning of the word 'squall' in a good dictionary.

17 (*a*) What sort of conditions are typical of a 'squall' (line 40)?

(*b*) What are the differences between a 'squall' and a 'shower'?

18 Why, at one point during the squall, might the ground appear 'blurry and swirling' (line 46)?

19 How does the writer convey the vividness of the scene when the setting sun suddenly shone on the plane and the flyers?

20 Why, do you think, would Christina feel that 'they were marooned in the sky like outcasts' (line 54)?

21 Look up the meaning of the word 'serpentine' (used as an adjective) in a good dictionary.

(*a*) What would 'serpentine turns' (line 56) look like if you were watching them?

(*b*) How would these movements differ from the 'tight

corkscrew descents' (line 61), do you think?

22   What would 'sodden pasture' (line 78) look and feel like?

C *Ideas for writing*

23   Write a story, true or imaginary, in which your adventures involve using a map and in which your eventual safety in fact depends on your being able to use that map accurately.

24   Unpleasant weather conditions helped to make Christina and Will's flight more difficult. Bad weather can sometimes make a journey, whether by land, sea or air, not only difficult but also dangerous. Write a description of a journey, real or imaginary, in which bad weather makes what should have been a routine trip both exciting and rather dangerous.

D *Suggestions for reading*

This passage comes from *The Edge of the Cloud*, the second of three books in the 'Flambards' trilogy by K.M. Peyton. Much of the book is concerned with the adventures and excitements of the pioneer days of designing and flying the early aeroplanes just before the outbreak of the First World War. You may prefer to start with the first book in the 'Flambards' series, *Flambards*. This is about five years in the childhood of Christina (who appears in the passage you have just read) at Flambards, a country house and estate much geared to horse riding and hunting. Follow on with *The Edge of the Cloud* and then, perhaps, read the third story, *Flambards in Summer*. In this last story Christina, now a young widow, returns to Flambards to face the challenge of building it into the sort of home she had always dreamed of its being.

All three 'Flambards' books are available in Puffin paperbacks.

There are plenty of good old-fashioned flying adventures to be found in the 'Biggles' books by Captain W.E. Johns. There are many of these books, including *Biggles and Co*, *Biggles and the Black Raider* and *Biggles Foreign Legionnaire*, available in Armada paperbacks.

15
The Daisy Dog's vigil

In ancient China, no one was allowed to own pekingese dogs except the Imperial family. Therefore, when in the 16th century the emperor wished to honour England's Elizabeth I, there was no greater gift he could bestow than a pair of the dogs he valued so highly. The bitch was placed in a carved ivory box, while the dog ran free. A royal princess was chosen to escort the animals across the world.

During the long and arduous journey, the bitch gave birth to five pups, and the little dog guarded his family in the ivory
10 box, and guarded the princess too. Finally, they reached France, and the princess found a Cornish ship to take them to England. But on the voyage across the Channel, the crew wove wild tales about their passenger; they said she was a slant-eyed demon, and the box she carried contained treasure.

When the vessel reached the Cornish coast, a storm arose, driving it towards the murderous cliffs. The frightened crew, blaming the impending disaster on the princess, burst into her cabin. One sailor tried to grab the box, but drew back with his hand bleeding from the little dog's bite. In terror, the crew
20 threw the princess overboard. The wind changed, and the ship veered to safety.

The girl's body and the box were washed into a lonely cove near Land's End. No one would approach the supposed devil on the beach except one man, a village simpleton, and he it was who discovered that the princess was dead. Only the dog remained alive, and it was dying. It watched the simpleton dig a grave in which he placed all the bodies together. Then he gathered wild daisies and planted them in the shape of a cross. Finally, he placed the little dog among the daisies, where it
30 licked his hand and died.

The ship reached harbour, and the tale of the treasure spread along the coast. But when the bitten man died, no one would go near the mound on the beach with the cross of daisies. It was said that a ghostly dog defended the lonely grave, and its bite was death. Perhaps it keeps its vigil still, for it is said that as late as 1850, a boy found a piece of carved ivory near the cliffs. As he picked it up, he felt himself bitten. Though his injuries were slight, the boy died; he had been bitten by the Daisy Dog, and was therefore doomed.

THE READER'S DIGEST ASSOCIATION LTD
Folklore, Myths and Legends of Britain

A Comprehension

1 What was the special position held by pekingese dogs in ancient China?

2 Why did the Chinese emperor decide to send a pekingese dog and bitch to Queen Elizabeth I?

3 Why did the crew of the Cornish ship taking the princess and the dogs from France to England think that the princess was 'a slant-eyed demon' and that the box contained treasure, do you think?

4 Why did the crew believe that the princess was responsible for the storm which threatened to wreck the ship?

5 (a) Why did the sailor try to grab the box?
(b) Why, perhaps, did they throw the princess overboard?
(c) What did the sailors probably think when the wind changed and the ship was able to continue safely?

6 Why, perhaps, did the dying pekingese dog not bite the village simpleton?

7 For what reasons would no one approach the grave mound on the beach in spite of the belief that the box in the grave contained treasure?

8 How did the death of the boy in Cornwall in 1850 add to people's belief in the truth of the legend of the Daisy Dog?

9 Why was the dog nicknamed the Daisy Dog?

10 What qualities in the Daisy Dog, both during its life and as a ghost dog, are revealed in this story?

B Interpretation and criticism

11 Look up the meaning of the word 'vigil' in a good dictionary.
Why is this story called 'The Daisy Dog's *vigil*'?

12 Look up the meaning of the word 'escort' in a good dictionary.
Why is the use of the word 'escort' more correct in the sentence 'A royal princess was chosen to *escort* the animals . . .' (line 6) than the word 'accompany'?

13 What qualities would you expect in an '*arduous* journey' (line 8), especially at the time described in this story?

14 Why are the cliffs on the Cornish coast described as 'murderous' (line 16)?

15 What is the situation when a disaster is 'impending' (line 17)?

16 'The ship veered to safety...' (line 20).
What does the use of the word 'veered' suggest about the closeness of the boat to disaster at that time?

17 (a) What would a typical 'cove' look like (line 22)?
(b) In what ways can a 'bay' be very different in appearance from a 'cove'?

18. (a) What kind of person is a 'simpleton' (line 24)?
(b) What qualities does the village simpleton in this story possess which underline the fact that fine feelings have nothing to do with intelligence?

19 How does the *sound* of the word 'doomed' (line 39) somehow reflect its meaning?

20 Why are stories about animals in general, and dogs in particular, so popular with both children and adults?

C Ideas for writing

21 Taking, perhaps, some of the following dramatic details found in the passage, write an exciting story set around a rocky coast like that of Cornwall at the present day:
'Wild tales' about a passenger on a ship or boat in distress.
A storm which is driving the ship towards 'murderous cliffs'.
A frightened crew.
A lonely cove.

22 Write a story, true or imaginary, which tells of the ways in which a dog shows great loyalty or bravery in guarding, defending or guiding his master or mistress.

D *Suggestions for reading*

This passage comes from a beautifully produced and illustrated book published by The Readers Digest Association, *Folklore, Myths and Legends of Britain*. It is taken from the section 'Romance of Britain', a guide to the strange folk stories and legends connected with the various regions of Britain. The book is ideal for dipping into, particularly in connection with the legends of your own area or of an area you plan to visit on holiday. There are many other short stories, like the one you have just read, in the book.

Books like this can be a pleasure just to *look* at before you decide on something definite to read in them. Several have been produced by Readers Digest/AA Publications; you will find plenty to look at and to read, for instance, in the *AA Book of the British Countryside*. You can read more legends in *The Book of Sea Legends*, a Puffin paperback edited by Michael Brown, and in a series of Puffin paperbacks by Roger Lancelyn Green which include *The Book of Dragons, The Book of Magicians, Myths of the Norsemen, Tales of Ancient Egypt* and *Tales of the Greek Heroes*.

16
Miss Crowle's strange encounter

Miss Mary Crowle did not scream when she thought she saw the ghost, she continued to play the organ. She was watching her fingers as they sidled over the keys, the white ivory yellow in the soft light above the keyboard. The church around her was dark, the Jacobean[1] pews creaking secrets to one another as they always did at night – not that Mary Crowle minded the night noises of Saint Mary's Danedyke.

She was practising Jeremiah Clarke's *Trumpet Voluntary*, which Jenny Jackson from the Home Farm had chosen for her
10 wedding march. She did not know the piece well, so when the last child had left the village school, she had hurried through tea and housework and come along in the dusk gathering over the tumbled tombstones of the churchyard to practise. She had had some difficulty with the complicated lock the Rector had fitted to the north door. But she had managed it, frowning and tutting a little. The previous Rector had only been interested in pigs. But then he had not spent more of his life as a policeman.

She had gone to the organ – as she always did – without bothering to turn on the lights. Her practised hand had found
20 the switch for the motor. It had sighed into life in the dark church. She had switched on the light over the keyboard and started to practise Jeremiah Clarke. She had put up her hand to turn the page of music, and her eye had gone over the top of the console[2] into the darkness beyond, where the shadows lay.

It was then that she saw the ghost.

Beyond the empty choir stalls, on the far side of the shadowy sanctuary, where the tiny flame of the sanctuary lamp flickered

[1] of the 17th century, particularly the reign of James 1st of England
[2] the desk from which the organ is played, containing the keyboard and the organ stops.

74

was the open door to the Relic Chapel. It was there that the
Danedyke Cup had once been kept, bringing pilgrims from the
30 four corners of medieval England. It was there that Abbot
John, the last abbot of the Benedictine Monastery, had been
found dead. It was there that his ghost walked – so village
tradition said. But Mary Crowle was fifty-five, and far too sensible to believe in village tales.

But the sanctuary lamp flickered, sending long shadows running up the walls and gleaming dully on the encaustic[1] tiles of
the sanctuary floor. And as the little flame gleamed momen-
tarily bright, through the open doorway, standing between the
chapel altar and Sir John Carruthers's tomb, Mary Crowle saw
40 a black and shadowy figure and the gleam of a white face. And
then it was gone.

Miss Crowle's fingers missed a note. She took her left hand
from the keyboard, settled her spectacles more firmly on her
nose, and continued to play, her heart pounding faster than
she would have cared to admit. She had been a sensible, utterly
devoted school teacher for thirty-five years, thirty of which she
had spent in Danedyke, and she did not believe in ghosts.
Anyway, she told herself firmly, no self-respecting ghost would
appear while someone was playing Jeremiah Clarke's *Trumpet*
50 *Voluntary*. It was far too cheerful, even if the church was dark
and what the children called 'spooky'.

She knew the legend about Abbot John well enough. She
even taught it to the children in school, hoping to help them to
love their parish church as she did herself. And it was a
touching legend. Abbot John had been ejected when the
monastery was suppressed and its treasures confiscated – including the Danedyke Cup, which was supposed to have
belonged to Mary, the mother of Jesus, and to have been
brought to England by Joseph of Arimathea. John had eked
60 out a miserable existence for some ten years and had then come
back to the stripped chapel which had housed the relic. There,
before the ruined shrine, where the altar had once stood, he
had been found dead. He was on his knees, his hands cold and
rigid, clasped in prayer.

Mary Crowle stopped playing because she had run out of
Jeremiah Clarke. She did *not* believe in ghosts. If there was a

[1] patterned by a burning process

75

being in the chapel, it was alive and human. Mentally she chided her thumping heart as if it was a wayward infant.

She picked up the English Hymnal, opened it and started to
70 play at random. The hymn was *Rock of Ages Cleft for Me.* And that was a tune suitable for a ghost. Solemn and sombre, it echoed through the empty church. Still playing, she stood up and peered across the top of the console, to the pointed shadow of the chapel door outlined by the flickering lamp. There was nothing to see but darkness. She sat down again, her fingers still playing.

> Could my soul no respite know,
> Could my tears for ever flow
> All for sin could not atone:
80 Thou must save, and thou alone.

She brought the hymm to a close and sat a moment, frowning, her fingers resting lightly on the keys, the only sound the whine of the organ motor.

This was quite ridiculous. Even if Abbot John had died as the legend said, in the chapel . . . well, all human beings had to die some time, and all the village tales about cowled monks and headless horsemen were as much nonsense here in the dark church as they were in her own bright parlour in the School House. Anyway she was a Christian.

90 Nothing in my hand I bring
> Simply to thy cross I cling.

She quoted the words to herself, because she had just been playing the tune. If there was anyone in the Relic Chapel it was someone belonging to the twentieth, not the sixteenth century. In fact it was probably Jimmy Bates. Jimmy was a naughty little boy, and he had an unhealthy interest in tombstones. In fact Jimmy had tried to remove the prayer book that the stone effigy of Sir John Carruthers was holding. He had done a great deal of expensive damage. Mary Crowle stooped down and
100 switched off the organ motor, a frown on her face as she thought of Jimmy, and the organ motor whined into silence. She stood up smiling. Jimmy Bates was not really naughty. Only very curious. And his father was a wastrel.

She went into the vestry and switched on the choir lights, watching over the curtain as the whitewashed walls, the painted memorials and the angels of the hammer beam roof came into view. She marched across in front of the altar rails, her sensible shoes clacking on the tiles. She made a little curtsey to the altar. She stood by the door into the Relic Chapel.

110 The interior was very black now that the choir and sanctuary were flooded with light. Her eyes behind the spectacles were screwed up because of the sudden brightness. Her heart was hardly pounding at all.

'Come out!' she said, her voice echoing down the dark nave in front of her. 'Jimmy Bates, come out this minute. You're being very naughty.'

There was silence. She paused a moment, realising soberly that she would find it very difficult to carry out the threat she was about to make. The interior of the chapel seemed so black.

120 She took a deep breath.

'If you don't come out,' she said firmly, 'I shall come in and turn the light on.'

Nothing happened.

'Very well,' said Miss Crowle and stepped into the dark doorway.

A shape came rushing at her out of the blackness and an arm lashed across her face, hurling her aside so that she fell backward with a scream over the altar rail, the oak rail crashing painfully into the small of her back.

130 She rolled over and struggled to a sitting position, leaning against the altar itself, conscious of both the pain in her back and the curious incongruity of sitting on the altar step with her skirts round her waist. As her eyes focused she saw a dark shadow vanish beyond the reach of the choir lights down the centre aisle. She could hear running feet, and then a fumbling, and then the north door opening, and then the crash as it closed.

She was shaking as she struggled to her feet, pulling herself up by the altar frontal. Her back was very painful, and she had

140 to retrieve her spectacles from the corner of the sanctuary. She stood with her hands on the altar and smiled weakly at the brass cross. At least it had not been a ghost. It had not been Jimmy Bates either.

STEPHEN CHANCE
Septimus and the Danedyke Mystery

77

A Comprehension

1 What evidence is there in the passage that Mary Crowle was used to going into the church after dark?

2 Why was she in church on this occasion?

3 How did she come to see what looked like a ghost when she was playing the organ?

4 For what reasons did she not stop playing when she saw the figure?

5 (a) In which part of the church was the figure when she saw it?

(b) Why might some villagers immediately have assumed that it *was* a ghost?

6 Discuss the various reasons why Miss Crowle decided to play a hymn.

7 (a) What conclusion did she come to about the figure she had seen?

(b) Why did she come to this conclusion?

8 (a) What action did she decide to take?

(b) What did her action prove to her in the end?

9 What evidence is there in the passage to suggest that Miss Crowle *was* a little frightened and that she was also a bit cross with herself for feeling frightened?

10 How did she go about *thinking* herself out of her fright?

11 What do you learn about Miss Crowle's character and personality from her behaviour in the church on this occasion?

B Interpretation and criticism

12 There are a number of interesting words connected with churches to be found in this passage. Use a good dictionary to find the meanings of the following words:

(a) *stall* (line 26). Trace the interesting origins of this word. How did it come to have the meaning it has here?

(b) *choir* (line 26). What are the two separate meanings of the word when used in connection with churches? Is there any relationship between the two meanings?

(c) *sanctuary* (line 27). Try to find the Latin root of the word. See if you can also find out what a *sanctuary lamp* (line 27) is and why it is kept alight.

(d) *chapel* (line 28). Note that this is a chapel *inside* a church. Try to find out why there are such chapels inside some churches.

(*e*) *relic* (line 28). What is the special meaning of the word as used here? What was the relic once kept in the Relic Chapel at Danedyke? Why was it regarded as a relic?

(*f*) *shrine* (line 62). Why was there *once* a shrine at Danedyke church?

(*g*) *vestry* (line 104). What connection might a vestry sometimes have with *vestments*?

(*h*) *nave* (line 114). Why would there be an echo down the nave when Miss Crowle called out?

(*i*) *effigy* (line 98). Why are effigies in churches likely to be connected with tombs?

13 (*a*) The children of the village considered Danedyke church to be 'spooky' (line 51). Bearing in mind what the words you have just been exploring have told you, discuss the reasons why churches containing features similar to those at Danedyke could seem 'spooky', particularly in poor light.

(*b*) What made Danedyke church *extra* 'spooky'?

14 How does the writer help to make the atmosphere of Danedyke church spooky for you, the reader?

15 In what ways does the writer's brief account of the legend of Abbot John and the Danedyke Cup add to the interest and the excitement of this passage?

16 How does the writer help you to share Miss Crowle's thoughts and feelings as she practises alone in the darkened church?

17 In what ways does the playing of the organ add to the tension of the passage? Could the passage have been as effective if Miss Crowle had only come into the church to arrange some flowers?

18 (*a*) This passage is the opening section of the *first* chapter of a detective story. Why might it encourage you to read on?

(*b*) Discuss some of the best opening chapters in books you have read, and explain why you have enjoyed them.

C *Ideas for writing*

19 Somewhere not far from your home there is almost certain-

ly an old building which you consider to be 'spooky'. Study this building carefully and then try writing the first chapter of an adventure story which begins with a strange happening in this building. Give your readers a detailed impression of the inside of the building in the same way the writer did in the passage you have just been studying.

20 Can you discover a legend or a true tale of the historical past connected with your home area? If you can, write it down briefly and then use it as the basis of a story in which you and your friends become involved in a present-day adventure strangely connected with the old legend or tale. If you can't discover a local legend make one up and then use it in your story.

D Suggestions for reading

This passage comes from an exciting detective novel by Stephen Chance entitled *Septimus and the Danedyke Mystery*. The story is set mostly around the church in the village of 'Danedyke' not far from Wisbech and in the heart of the lonely Fen country of Eastern England. The vicar of Danedyke, the Reverend Septimus Treloar, used to be a detective, and after the attack on Miss Crowle his old interests are instantly revived as he sets out to discover why violent intruders are so interested in the Relic Chapel. Septimus is soon involved in some creepy night watches inside the church, and the story moves to a dramatic climax set on a boat heading down one of the Fenland waterways and out to sea with Septimus in the clutches of the villains!

Septimus and the Danedyke Mystery is published as a Puffin paperback. You can read another of Septimus's adventures as a vicar turned detective in *Septimus and the Minster Ghost*, also available as a Puffin paperback.

Notes on authors

BAWDEN, Nina

Like Carrie, in her novel, *Carrie's War*, Nina Bawden was evacuated to South Wales from London at the outbreak of the Second World War. She remembers her own childhood clearly and her recollections of often having felt bad and wicked as a child have influenced the way she has written about children. She felt that the children in the books *she* read as a child never seemed to possess 'the dark and angry feelings' which she had experienced – and which she eventually realised were experienced by all children. She decided that her books for children would explore feelings which children would recognise as being true. Many of Nina Bawden's children's books have been serialised for BBC television (notably *Carrie's War* and *The Peppermint Pig*) and read as serials on BBC television's *Jackanory*. She has also written a number of successful novels for adults, including *Afternoon of a Good Woman*, which reflects her experience of being a Justice of the Peace sitting in both adult and juvenile courts.

CHAMBERS, Aidan

Aidan Chambers was born and brought up in County Durham and members of his family included miners, an undertaker and a footman. After spending two years in the Royal Navy he trained as a teacher and taught for eleven years in Secondary Schools. He also spent seven years as an Anglican monk. He wanted, however, to be a writer and in 1968 he achieved his ambition of becoming a full-time writer. In the 1970s he published, with his wife, 'Signal', a magazine devoted to children's books and became General Editor of Macmillan's popular series of paperbacks for schools, *Topliners*, as well as becoming an established writer of children's books which have included *Breaktime*, a novel for adolescents.

CHANCE, Stephen

Stephen Chance is a pen-name and we now know that, like Septimus in *Septimus and the Danedyke Mystery*, he is a clergyman, the Rev Philip Turner, an Anglican priest. The Rev Philip Turner is a writer of children's books and his novel *The Grange at High Force* won the Carnegie Medal in 1965. His father and mother were born in Peterborough and the Fenland settings of *Septimus and the Danedyke Mystery* reflect his intimate knowledge of the area gained from holidays spent exploring the Fen country and, in particular, the many inspiring churches of Fenland – churches like that at 'Danedyke'.

His richly varied life has included an initial spell as a mechanical engineer after the Second World War, followed by work in H M Prisons, youth work, and hospital administration before periods as a parish priest and as a member of the BBC's Religious Department. After a spell at Eton as a chaplain he has taught in both comprehensive and public schools, but he now concentrates more on his writing and, by 1979, 'Stephen Chance' had written three books about his clergyman-detective, Septimus, the latest being *Septimus and the Stone Offering*, an exciting story set in Wales.

CLARKE, Arthur C.

Arthur C. Clarke was born in Minehead, Somerset, in 1917. During the Second World War he served in the RAF and was a Radar Instructor and Technical Officer in the first Ground Controlled Approach radar. He originated the proposals for the first use of satellites for communications. After the war he took a first class B.Sc. degree in physics and mathematics.

Since 1954 he has been engaged in his hobby of underwater exploration and photography of the Great Barrier Reef of Australia and the coast of Sri Lanka. He was a commentator for American CBS television on the moon flights of Apollo 11, 12 and 15. He has been responsible for the salvaging of a treasure-filled man-of-war.

He is one of the major world writers of science fiction and his novels have won him many awards. One of his most famous stories, *2001: A Space Odyssey*, was made into a memorable film. He and Stanley Kubrick were jointly nominated for an Oscar for their screenplay of this film.

The many scientific associations of which he has been chairman include the British Interplanetary Society, the Royal Astronomical Society, the American Rocket Society, and the British Sub-Aqua Club. He has lived in Sri Lanka since 1956.

KILNER, Geoffrey

Geoffrey Kilner is a Yorkshireman who was born and went to school in Barnsley before going up to Oxford University. He is a lecturer in further education and was, in 1979, living in Herefordshire with his wife and three children. *Jet, a Gift to the Family*, published in 1976, was his first novel and it was a runner-up for the Kestrel-Guardian Award in 1975.

PATCHETT, Mary Elwyn
The wide knowledge of the wild life of the Australian bush revealed in Mary Elwyn Patchett's books was acquired at first hand during her early life. She was born close to the border of New South Wales and Queensland in an area then in the heart of the Australian bush. The loneliness of her childhood spent with her pets and half-tame bush creatures is described in the *Ajax* books; which include *Ajax the Warrior*. The love of animals acquired during her bush childhood has inspired many of her stories, notably those featuring the wild horses of the brumby herd in *The Brumby*, and its sequels.
Mary Elwyn Patchett took up full-time writing as a career after coming to London. Before that she had worked as a journalist in Australia for a number of years.

PEYTON, K.M.
K.M. Peyton was born in 1929 and starting writing when she was nine. Her first book was published in 1947 when she was still at school. Her husband is a freelance commercial artist specialising in sailing subjects. Mrs Peyton left teaching in the late 1950s to devote herself to full-time writing. Her major break-through as a writer of children's books came with the success of her novel of sea adventure, *Windfall*, published in 1963. In her early sailing days she had many frights and she claims that 'to be really frightened, to the extent that one thinks one is going to die – is a very useful experience for the novelist.' According to Mrs Peyton, Christina's experiences in being introduced into the male world of flying in the 'Flambards' novel *The Edge of the Cloud*, paralleled her own experiences in being introduced into the male world of sailing. Her interest in the pioneer days of flying before the First World War had been fired when she had been researching for information in connection with a scene in an earlier book, *Thunder in the Sky*. She enjoyed writing the 'flying machine' episodes in *Flambards* so much that she decided to explore the possibilities of extending the subject of pioneer aviation in another book – which became the second in the 'Flambards' trilogy – *The Edge of the Cloud*.

POTTS, Richard
Richard Potts has led a varied existence. He was born in York and left school at sixteen. After spending four years as an apprentice draughtsman and undertaking National Service as a Nursing Orderly in the RAF he went on to take a degree at Keele University. He lived for a time in Cornwall before returning to York to teach. He is married to a folk singer, Alison McMorland, and they have three children. *A Boy and His Bike* was Richard Potts's third book written for children. His earlier book, *The Haunted Mine*, was featured on BBC television's *Jackanory* as a serial.

SAVILLE, Malcolm

Malcolm Saville, born in Hastings, Sussex, in 1901, has been an extremely popular writer of children's adventure stories for very many years. As well as being the author of many adventure novels, notably the series of stories of the Lone Pine Club, Malcolm Saville contributed extensively to BBC Radio *Children's Hour* for many years prior to its succumbing to the competition of children's television and he was also for many years a contributor to the popular and long-established *Children's Newspaper* until it ceased publication. Malcolm Saville welcomed contact with his readers, encouraging them to write and tell them what they thought of his books when they read them in paperback, and promising to answer their letters.

STORR, Catherine

Catherine Storr was born in London and has lived there for most of her life. She is a qualified doctor and she worked as a doctor for fourteen years before giving up her work in order to have time for writing. Her first books such as *Stories for Jane* (1952) were written for younger children – for her own three young daughters, in fact. Later, as her daughters grew up, her novels were written for older children – *Marianne Dreams*, for instance, and for adolescents – notably *Marianne and Mark* and *Thursday*. Now, with her daughters grown up, she writes also for adults. She believes, however, that she will always want to go on writing for children because they share her enjoyment of a story and because they are able to appreciate stories in which – as in *Marianne Dreams* and *Thursday* – the world of the imagination is as real as the world of actual everyday happenings.

STUCLEY, Elizabeth

When Elizabeth Stucley lived in the Clapham Common area of South London, she founded The Adventurers' Club for the boys and girls of the neighbourhood. Their activities included play-acting, painting, and camping. They were the inspiration for her novel *Magnolia Buildings*, from which the passage 'The Bonfire' has been taken. In this novel Ally, eldest of the four children in the Berners family, found some much-needed adventure in her life when she took part in the school Christmas pantomime and acted everyone else off the stage! Elizabeth Stucley was born in 1906 and died in 1974. During the Second World War she was a volunteer driver for the French Army and was mentioned in despatches. She later became Headmistress of St Cuthbert's School and she was a social worker. Although she wrote for both adults and children, she became particularly concerned about underprivileged children and it was, in particular, the writing of *Magnolia Buildings* which made her sensitively aware of the lives and the problems of 'block dwellers' – perhaps because she had led such a widely-travelled life, full of experience, herself.

THOMAS, Leslie

Leslie Thomas was born in Newport, South Wales, in 1931. After the deaths of both his parents he spent his childhood and youth at Dr Barnardo's Home in Kingston-upon-Thames, Surrey, and it was during his time there that he decided that he wanted to be a writer. Apart from spending two years in the Army doing National Service between 1949 and 1951, he worked for a number of years as a journalist in the London area between 1948 and 1966, first with local newspapers and later as a special writer for the *London Evening News*. In 1964 he wrote *This Time Next Week*, which described his childhood and his life as a Barnardo Boy. His major breakthrough came, however, with the publication of his richly entertaining novel *The Virgin Soldiers* in 1966. Since then he has produced a succession of best-selling popular novels which have enjoyed record sales in paperbacks. He now lives quietly on the edge of the New Forest, in Hampshire, continuing with his writing, and having successfully achieved his early ambition.

UTTLEY, Alison

Just like Susan in *The Country Child*, Alison Uttley spent her childhood on a remote farm in the Derbyshire hills, a farm which had belonged to generations of ancestors. The family was not wealthy, but her mother always bought books when she could spare the money, and they were happy making their own music and entertainments. Like Susan, Alison Uttley had to walk two miles to her first school in a small Derbyshire hamlet. There, lessons in geology fired her interest in science, and eventually, after going to grammar school, she went to Manchester University and gained an honours degree in physics and advanced mathematics. She taught for a time and then married. She gained her first experiences of story-telling through the many stories she made up for her one son. After the death of her husband she began to write and her autobiographical story *The Country Child* was her first book. Then followed many of her famous stories for young children, including the well-known *Adventures of Sam Pig*.

WELLS, H.G.

H.G. Wells's early life provided material for his novels. His father ran a small crockery shop in Bromley, Kent, and H.G. Wells also worked for a time as a draper's apprentice and as a chemist's apprentice. His shop experiences and his childhood inspired two of his most well-known and comic novels, *Kipps* and *The History of Mr Polly*. His experiences as a chemist's apprentice provided ideas for his novel *Tono-Bungay*, 'Tono-Bungay' being a patent medicine offering Health, Beauty and Strength! Later, Wells became a schoolmaster for a time, and his experiences provided material for his novel *Love and Mr Lewisham*.

He took up writing as his main occupation in 1893 and in 1895 achieved his first major success with his first full-length novel, the science fiction story *The Time Machine*. Previously, Wells had studied for his bachelor of science degree and his interest in science had been fired by his period of study under Thomas Huxley, the brilliant 19th century biologist.

WILDER, Laura Ingalls

The Little House in the Big Woods, Little House on the Prairie, On the Banks of Plum Creek: the titles of three of Laura Ingalls Wilder's books point to the homes of her childhood. Laura Ingalls was very much part of the great movement West by many American families in the second half of the 19th century. She was born in a log cabin in Wisconsin in 1867 – 'the little house in the big woods'. With her parents and her sister Mary she travelled by covered wagon into Indian Territory and lived in 'the little house on the prairie'. Then, still travelling by covered wagon, they moved to western Minnesota, where they lived for a few years 'on the banks of Plum Creek'.

At 15, Laura Ingalls started to train as a teacher. Three years later she married Almanzo Wilder and they had one child, Rose. After travelling around for a number of years they settled in Missouri. When Rose grew up she remembered all the stories her mother had told her about her childhood experiences, and urged her mother to write a book about them. *The Little House in the Big Woods* was published in 1932 and Laura Ingalls Wilder went on to write another nine books about her pioneering days. She died in 1957 at the age of ninety.